MUHAMMAD ALI

IN PERSPECTIVE

THOMAS HAUSER

WITH THE COOPERATION OF MUHAMMAD ALI

 CollinsPublishersSanFrancisco
A Division of HarperCollins*Publishers*

AN OPUS BOOK

For Lonnie Ali, a woman of exceptional integrity, intelligence, and grace

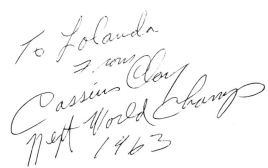

When I first saw Muhammad, I can remember exactly what he looked like. I can see it now. He had

that wonderful smile, and he was very clean-cut. He was wearing dark trousers, a white shirt, and

a black bow tie. He put me on his lap. And Muhammad has these standard lines that he says to

little girls — "You sure are pretty. What's your name?" That kind of thing. I don't know how much

I answered him, because I was very shy and scared to death. But I remember it all very well, and it's

quite special to me that someone actually took a photo of us together that day.

- - - - - - - - - - -

LONNIE ALI

Published by Collins Publishers San Francisco, a division of Harper Collins Publishers.

Created and produced by Opus Productions Inc. 300 West Hastings Street, Vancouver, British Columbia, Canada V6B 1K6

Copyright ©1996 by Muhammad Ali, Thomas Hauser, and Opus Productions Inc.

Library of Congress Cataloging-in-Publication Data:
Hauser, Thomas.
        Muhammad Ali in perspective / Thomas Hauser with the cooperation of Muhammad Ali.
        p.   cm.
        ISBN 0-00-225189-2
        1. Ali, Muhammad, 1942- . 2. Boxers (Sports) — United States — Biography. I. Ali, Muhammad, 1942- . II. Title
GV1132.A44H39 1996
796.8'3'092—dc20
[B]   96-20998
                                                                             CIP

10 9 8 7 6 5 4 3 2 1

As I sit down to write this foreword, I have just returned home from the 1996 Centennial Olympic Games in Atlanta. This time — as at the 1960 Rome Olympics — I was a participant, not a spectator.

Very few people knew about it at the time, but a month ago I was told by the Atlanta Committee for the Olympic Games that I had been chosen for the honor of lighting the cauldron that would signal the start of the 1996 Olympics. When Janet Evans carried her torch up the ramp inside the stadium, the whole world thought she would be the one to light the cauldron. Then I came into view for the passing of the flame and lit it. I hope the crowd, and the whole world, was as pleased as I was. It was an incredible thrill and honor for me to be at the center of this great event that was watched by more than three billion people.

Lighting the Olympic flame brought back a lot of memories for me. In 1960, I was young, confident, and by my own standards, very handsome. But not many people knew who I was. Then I won a gold medal in boxing at the Rome Olympics, and my life began to change. Now, thirty-six years later, I'm still handsome, but many things are different. And I have a lot to be thankful for. God has blessed me in many ways. I've lived a life that was once beyond my imagination even to dream about. I've been heavyweight champion of the world three times. I've had the opportunity to speak out against a war that I thought was morally wrong. I've been privileged to stand up for people who are oppressed because of their religion and the color of their skin. And I feel like the most loved person in the world.

As I've grown older, I've also become a much more spiritual person than I was when I was young. I now believe that the life we lead on Earth is but a mosquito's wing compared to eternity and life in the hereafter. And I've learned that whatever time we spend on Earth should be spent helping others and creating justice and equality for all people; not out of pity or shame, but out of love for all people with the knowledge that we belong, not to many races but to one race — the human race.

The photographs and thoughts in this book are a reflection of my life. Some of them come from friends and family members who have been with me for many years. Others are from people who have observed me from a distance. Some of the names and faces in this book are easily recognized. Others are not. I hope you enjoy the book and learn from it. And I hope that, like the Olympic flame, my life will light up the world with hope and love for all people. That, to me, is the true meaning of my life when I put it "In Perspective."

Muhammad Ali

Muhammad Ali
Berrien Springs, Michigan

Mike Katz, one of America's best boxing writers, once said that Muhammad Ali was more accessible to the media than any athlete he'd ever known. "He accepted writers as part of his world," Katz noted. "And not just reporters from the major newspapers and television stations. Ali would spend as much time talking to a tenth-grader from the local high school newspaper as he would to the boxing writer for the *New York Times.*"

Katz's words rang true to me, because I've experienced that part of Ali firsthand. In 1967, when Muhammad was preparing to fight Zora Folley, I was a student at Columbia University. Several days before the fight, I went to Madison Square Garden to tape an interview with Ali for Columbia's student-run radio station. I watched Ali go through a series of training exercises. Then I looked on from the edge of the ring as he sparred for several rounds. And when the time for interviews came, Ali spent as much time with me as he did with any of the media giants on hand.

Two decades later, I was reunited with Ali in a more meaningful role. Muhammad and his wife, Lonnie, asked if I'd be interested in authoring "the definitive Ali biography," and *Muhammad Ali: His Life And Times* was born. It has occurred to me often since then that I was in the right place at the right time. I had total access to Muhammad and those around him. I enjoyed the advantage of being able to view his accomplishments with a degree of perspective not available to authors who'd written about him in earlier times. And I was fortunate in that, when I began writing, all of the people central to Ali's life were still alive with the exception of Sonny Liston and Bundini Brown.

But times change; events go on. More than a dozen of the people I interviewed for *Muhammad Ali: His Life And Times* have died. Both of Muhammad's parents have passed away since then, although their influence upon him remains strong. Other deaths that have been noted with sadness include Lana Shabazz, John Condon, Luis Sarria, C.B. Atkins, Howard Cosell, Wilma Rudolph, Harold Conrad, Alex Haley, Bob Surkein, Barney Nagler, Joe Ingraham, Erwin Griswold, and Marvin Kohn. Still, even as people important to Ali die, others who he loves are born. In recent years, Muhammad has become a grandfather twice over. His youngest child, Asaad Amin, is now five years old. And Ali keeps growing; new things keep happening to him. Thus, *Muhammad Ali: In Perspective*, which adds to what has been written about Ali in the past and incorporates Ali's favorite images of himself, including most prominently photographs by Howard Bingham, who has been Ali's closest friend for more than thirty years.

Writing a book of this nature necessitates saying "thank you" many times. As always, I'm grateful to Muhammad and Lonnie Ali and Howard Bingham for their friendship and support. I also owe thanks to the following individuals who granted interviews specifically for this book: Seth Abraham, Teddy Atlas, Michael Bentt, Ron Borges, Ralph Boston, Marion Boykin, Ramsey Clark, Lou DiBella, Craig Hamilton, Jerry Izenberg, Roy Jones Jr., Mike Katz, Dave Kindred, Wally Mathews, William Nack, Ferdie Pacheco, and Roger Wilkins. This list does not include the hundreds of people I interviewed previously for *Muhammad Ali: His Life And Times* and with whom I've shared "the Ali watch" in recent years.

The sources for the written content of this book also include extensive archival material such as newspapers, magazines, and tapes. At times, I've joined separate quotations from the same speaker and excerpted statements to facilitate reporting on a particular thought or event. I'm confident that, in so doing, I've done nothing to distort what was said or otherwise compromise the fairness of the manuscript. And of course, I've also drawn upon my own personal observations, having seen Muhammad create new memories and generate "new material" that is funny, poignant, and warm.

By way of example, several years ago, I was with Ali in Seattle to attend a dinner where he was honored as "The Fighter of the Century." The festivities included a fight card at The Kingdome. And meeting Muhammad, the undercard fighters were in awe. One of them — a lightweight with a losing record in a handful of professional bouts — went so far as to confess, "Mr. Ali, I just want you to know: when I'm going to the ring for a fight, I get real nervous. So I say to myself, 'I'm Muhammad Ali; I'm the greatest fighter of all time, and no one can beat me.' "

Muhammad leaned toward the fighter and whispered, "When I was boxing and got nervous before a fight, I said the same thing."

Thomas Hauser
New York, N.Y.

PART ONE

THE IMPORTANCE OF MUHAMMAD ALI

Cassius Marcellus Clay, Jr., as Muhammad Ali was once known, was born in Louisville, Kentucky, on

January 17, 1942. Louisville was a city with segregated public facilities, noted for the Kentucky Derby, mint

juleps, and other reminders of southern aristocracy. Blacks were the servant class in Louisville. They raked

manure in the backstretch at Churchill Downs and cleaned other people's homes. Growing up in Louisville, the

best on the socioeconomic ladder that most black people could realistically hope for was to become a

clergyman or a teacher at an all-black public school. In a society where it was often felt that might makes right,

"white" was synonymous with both.

FACING PAGE: *In 1962, the young man who would become Muhammad Ali was still searching for his identity.*

ABOVE: *Four-year-old Cassius Clay posed with his younger brother, Rudolph, in this earliest-known photograph of "The Greatest."*

I weighed 89 pounds, and he weighed about the same. The fight was three rounds, a minute a round. And he hit me a whole lot more than I hit him. I had a heck of a headache that night. He won by a split decision. And right after he was announced the winner by the referee, he started shouting that he was going to be the greatest fighter ever. He was heavyweight champion of the world already, at twelve years old and 89 pounds.

RONNIE O'KEEFE

(CASSIUS CLAY'S OPPONENT IN HIS FIRST AMATEUR FIGHT. IT WAS THE ONLY FIGHT OF O'KEEFE'S RING CAREER.)

Ali's father, Cassius Marcellus Clay, Sr., supported a wife and two sons by painting billboards and signs. Ali's mother, Odessa Grady Clay, worked on occasion as a household domestic. "I remember one time when Cassius was small," Mrs. Clay later recalled, "we were downtown at a five-and-ten-cents store. He wanted a drink of water, and they wouldn't give him one because of his color. And that really affected him. He didn't like that at all, being a child and thirsty. He started crying, and I said, 'Come on; I'll take you someplace and get you some water.' But it really hurt him."

When Cassius Clay was twelve years old, his bike was stolen. That led him to take up boxing under the tutelage of a Louisville policeman named Joe Martin. Clay advanced through the amateur ranks, won a gold medal at the 1960 Olympics in Rome, and turned pro under the guidance of The Louisville Sponsoring Group, a syndicate comprised of eleven wealthy white men.

"Cassius was something in those days," his longtime physician, Ferdie Pacheco, remembers. "He began training in Miami with Angelo Dundee, and Angelo put him in a den of iniquity called the Mary Elizabeth Hotel, because Angelo is one of the most innocent men in the world and it was a cheap hotel. This place was full of pimps, thieves, and drug dealers. And here's Cassius, who comes from a good home, and all of a sudden he's involved with this circus of street people. At first, the hustlers thought he was just another guy to take to the cleaners; another guy to steal from; another guy to sell dope to; another guy to fix up with a girl. He had this incredible innocence about him, and usually that kind of person gets eaten alive in the ghetto. But then the hustlers all fell in love with him, like everybody does, and they started to feel protective of him. If someone tried to sell him a girl, the others would say, 'Leave him alone; he's not into that.' If a guy came around, saying, 'Have a drink,' it was, 'Shut up; he's in training.' But that's the story of Ali's life. He's always been like a little kid, climbing out onto tree limbs, sawing them off behind him, and coming out okay."

In the early stages of his professional career, Cassius Clay was more highly regarded for his charm and personality than for his ring skills. He told the world that he was "The Greatest," but the brutal realities of boxing seemed to dictate otherwise. Then, on February 25, 1964, in one of the most stunning upsets in sports history, Clay knocked out Sonny Liston to become heavyweight champion of the world. Two days later, he shocked the world again by announcing that he had accepted the teachings of a black separatist religion known as the Nation of Islam. And on March 6, 1964, he took the name "Muhammad Ali," which was given to him by his spiritual mentor, Elijah Muhammad.

For the next three years, Ali dominated boxing as thoroughly and magnificently as any fighter ever. But outside the ring, his persona was being sculpted in ways that were even more important. "My first impression of Cassius Clay," author Alex Haley later recalled, "was of someone with an incredibly versatile personality. You never knew quite where he was in psychic posture. He was almost like that shell game, with a pea and three shells. You know; which shell is the pea under? But he had a belief in himself and convictions far stronger than anybody dreamed he would."

As the sixties grew more tumultuous, Ali became a lightning rod for the turmoil and discontent that marked America. His message of black pride and black resistance to white domination was on the cutting edge of the era. Not everything he preached was wise, and Ali himself now rejects some of the beliefs that he adhered to then. Indeed, one might find an allegory for his life in a remark he once made to fellow Olympian Ralph Boston. "I played golf," Ali reported. "And I hit the thing long, but I never knew where it was going."

FACING PAGE: *At age twelve — the first boxing photo of the most famous fighter, and most famous athlete, of all time.*

Sometimes, though, Ali knew precisely where he was going. On April 28, 1967, citing his religious beliefs, he refused induction into the United States Army at the height of the war in Vietnam. Ali's refusal followed a blunt statement, voiced fourteen months earlier — "I ain't got no quarrel with them Vietcong." And the American establishment responded with a vengeance, demanding, "Since when did war become a matter of personal quarrels? War is duty. Your country calls; you answer."

On June 20, 1967, Ali was convicted of refusing induction into the United States Armed Forces and sentenced to five years in prison. Four years later, his conviction was unanimously overturned by the United States Supreme Court. But in the interim, he was stripped of his title and precluded from fighting for three and a half years. "He did not believe he would ever fight again," Ali's wife at that time, Belinda Ali, said later of her husband's "exile" from boxing. "He wanted to, but he truly believed that he would never fight again."

Meanwhile, Ali's impact was growing — among black Americans; among those who opposed the war in Vietnam; among all people with grievances against The System. "It's hard to imagine that a sports figure could have so much political influence on so many people," observes civil rights activist Julian Bond. And Jerry Izenberg of the *Newark Star-Ledger* recalls the scene in October 1970, when at long last Ali was allowed to return to the ring. "About two days before the fight against Jerry Quarry, it became clear to me that something had changed," Izenberg remembers. "Long lines of people were checking into the hotel. They were dressed differently than the people who used to go to fights. I saw men wearing capes and hats with plumes, and women wearing next to nothing at all. Limousines were lined up at the curb. Money was being flashed everywhere. And I was confused, until a friend of mine who was black said to me, 'You don't get it. Don't you understand? This is the heavyweight champion who beat The Man. The Man said he would never fight again, and here he is, fighting in Atlanta, Georgia.' "

Four months later, Ali's comeback was temporarily derailed when he lost to Joe Frazier. It was a fight of truly historic proportions. Nobody in America was neutral that night. "It does me good to lose about once every ten years," Ali jested after the bout. But physically and psychologically, his pain was enormous. Subsequently, Ali avenged his loss to Frazier twice in memorable bouts. And ultimately, he won the heavyweight championship of the world an unprecedented three times.

Meanwhile, Ali's religious views were evolving. In the mid-seventies, he began studying the Qur'an more seriously, focusing on Orthodox Islam. His earlier adherence to the teachings of Elijah Muhammad — that white people are "devils" and there is no heaven or hell — was replaced by a spiritual embrace of all people and preparation for his own afterlife. In 1984, Ali spoke out publicly against the separatist doctrine of Nation of Islam spokesman Louis Farrakhan, declaring, "What he teaches is not at all what we believe in. He represents the time of our struggle in the dark and a time of confusion in us, and we don't want to be associated with that at all." Ali today is a deeply religious man. Although his health is not what it once was, his thought processes remain clear. He is, still, the most recognizable and the most loved person in the world.

FACING PAGE. TOP: *Cassius Clay (top row, far left) and Jimmy Ellis (between Clay and coach Joe Martin) were among the eight amateurs who represented Louisville in the 1959 Tournament of Champions in Chicago.* BOTTOM: *Among the fans who greeted gold-medal winner Cassius Clay at the airport when he returned from the 1960 Olympics were his parents and brother.*

I was fighting an Italian in Rome for the gold medal, so I figured my chances were not too

good. But I went out and beat Carmello Bosce of Italy. I beat him in the last round, and I came

back to the dressing room, shouting, "I got it! I got it! I got it!" Eddie Crook had to go out next.

Eddie went out, and he came back, shouting "I got it! I got it! I got it!" Eddie was hysterical.

He looked like a seven-year-old kid, he was so joyful. And Cassius, he was no nonsense. He

was getting ready to go out, concentrating on his objective. Then he went out, got his gold,

came back in; and we hugged each other and jumped up and down, and screamed and

screamed and screamed. We just couldn't believe it.

WILBERT "SKEETER" McCLURE

(CASSIUS CLAY'S ROOMMATE AND FELLOW GOLD MEDALIST AT THE 1960 OLYMPIC GAMES)

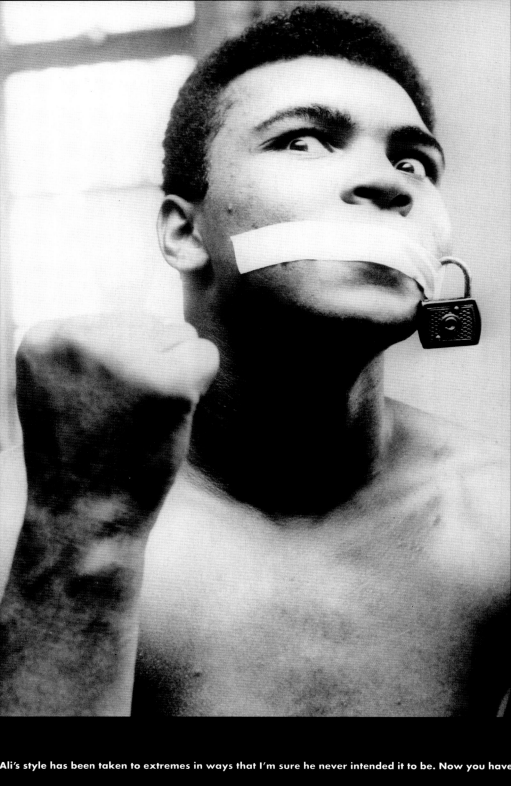

Ali's style has been taken to extremes in ways that I'm sure he never intended it to be. Now you have

boastfulness and bragging, but with no sense of irony and no principles behind it. These guys —

Deion Sanders, Barry Bonds, all of them — they just don't get it. Ali was the best "sound bite" in

history. Ali was "prime time" before Deion Sanders was born. Ali did that schtick better than anyone,

but with Ali, there was social relevance and substance behind it.

But is Muhammad Ali relevant today? In an age when self-dealing and greed have become public policy, does a man in his mid-fifties who suffers from Parkinson's Syndrome really matter? At a time when an intrusive worldwide electronic media dominates, and celebrity status and fame are mistaken for heroism, is true heroism possible?

In response to these questions, it should first be noted that, unlike many famous people, Ali is not a creation of the media. He used the media in extraordinary fashion. And certainly, he came along at the right time in terms of television. In 1960, when Cassius Clay won an Olympic gold medal, TV was crawling out of its infancy. The television networks had just learned how to focus cameras on people, build them up, and follow stories through to the end. And Ali loved that. As Jerry Izenberg later observed, "Once Ali found out about television, it was, 'Where? Bring the cameras! I'm ready now.' "

Still, Ali's fame is pure. Athletes today are known as much for their endorsement contracts and salaries as for their competitive performances. Fame now often stems from sports marketing rather than the other way around. Bo Jackson was briefly one of the most famous men in America because of his Nike (or was it Reebok?) shoe commercials. Michael Jordan and virtually all of his brethren derive a substantial portion of their visibility from commercial endeavors. Yet, as great an athlete as Michael Jordan is, he doesn't have the ability to move people's hearts and minds the way that Ali has moved them for decades. And what Muhammad Ali means to the world can be viewed from an ever deepening perspective today.

Ali entered the public arena as an athlete. And to many, that's significant. "Sports is a major factor in ideological control," says sociologist Noam Chomsky. "After all, people have minds; they've got to be involved in something; and it's important to make sure they're involved in things that have absolutely no significance. So professional sports is perfect. It instills the right ideas of passivity. It's a way of keeping people diverted from issues like who runs society and who makes the decisions on how their lives are to be led."

But Ali broke the mold. When he appeared on the scene, it was popular among those in the vanguard of the civil rights movement to take the "safe" path. That path wasn't safe for many of those who participated in the struggle. Martin Luther King, Jr., Medgar Evers, Viola Liuzzo, and other courageous men and women were subjected to economic assaults, violence, and death when they carried the struggle "too far." But the road they traveled was designed to be as non-threatening as possible for white America. White Americans were told, "All that black people want is what you want for yourselves. We're appealing to your conscience."

Then along came Ali, preaching not "white American values," but freedom and equality of a kind rarely seen anywhere in the world. And as if that wasn't threatening enough, Ali attacked the status quo from outside of politics and outside of the accepted strategies of the civil rights movement. "I remember when Ali joined the Nation of Islam," Julian Bond recalls. "The act of joining was not something many of us particularly liked. But the notion he'd do it; that he'd jump out there, join this group that was so despised by mainstream America, and be proud of it, sent a little thrill through you."

"The nature of the controversy," football great Jim Brown, also the founder of the Black Economic Union, said later, "was that white folks could not stand free black folks. White America could not stand to think that a sports hero

FACING PAGE: *"The Louisville Lip" was rarely silent in public. But unlike many superstars, Clay had the ability to laugh at himself.*

that it was allowing to make big dollars would embrace something like the Nation of Islam. But this young man had the courage to stand up like no one else and risk, not only his life, but everything else that he had."

Ali himself downplayed his role. "I'm not no leader. I'm a little humble follower," he said in 1964. But to many, he was the ultimate symbol of black pride and black resistance to an unjust social order. Sometimes Ali spoke with humor. "I'm not just saying black is best because I'm black," he told a college audience during his exile from boxing. "I can prove it. If you want some rich dirt, you look for the black dirt. If you want the best bread, you want the whole wheat rye bread. Costs more money, but it's better for your digestive system. You want the best sugar for cooking; it's the brown sugar. The blacker the berry, the sweeter the fruit. If I want a strong cup of coffee, I'll take it black. The coffee gets weak if I integrate it with white cream."

Other times, Ali's remarks were less humorous and more barbed. But for millions of people, being black took on a whole new meaning because of Ali. Listen to the voices of some who heard his call:

- Reggie Jackson: *Muhammad Ali gave me the gift of self-respect.*

- Hosea Williams: *Ali made you feel good about yourself. He made you feel so glad you are who you are; that God had made you black.*

- Bryant Gumbel: *One of the reasons the civil rights movement went forward was that black people were able to overcome their fear. And I honestly believe that, for many black Americans, that came from watching Muhammad Ali. He simply refused to be afraid. And being that way, he gave other people courage.*

- Alex Haley: *We are not white, you know. And it's not an anti-white thing to be proud to be us and to want someone to champion us. And Muhammad Ali was the absolute ultimate champion.*

- Dick Gregory: *Ali lived a lot of lives for a lot of people. And he was able to tell white folks for us to go to hell; that I'm going to do it my way.*

- Arthur Ashe: *This man helped give an entire people a belief in themselves and the will to make themselves better. But Ali didn't just change the image that African-Americans have of themselves. He opened the eyes of a lot of white people to the potential of African-Americans; who we are and what we can be.*

Abraham Lincoln once said that he regarded the Emancipation Proclamation as the central act of his administration. "It is a momentous thing," Lincoln wrote, "to be the instrument under Providence of the liberation of a race." Muhammad Ali was such an instrument. As commentator Gil Noble later explained, "Everybody was plugged into this man, because he was taking on America. There had never been anybody in his position who directly addressed himself to racism. Racism was virulent, but you didn't talk about those things. If you wanted to make it in this country, you had to be quiet, carry yourself in a certain way, and not say anything about what was going on, even though there was a knife sticking in your chest. Well, Ali changed all of that. He just laid it out and talked about racism and slavery and all of that stuff. He put it on the table. And everybody who was black, whether they said it overtly or covertly, said 'AMEN.' "

But Ali's appeal would come to extend far beyond black America. When he refused induction into the

FACING PAGE: *Cassius Clay looked on with approval as some Miami Beach locals helped promote his first fight against Sonny Liston.*

His independence was of a different order of independence; almost inherent, as if he was born that way. I'll bet you anything that, when he was five years old, he was like that. He just did what he thought he ought to do. He wasn't born to be forced; he's a totally independent human being. And to some people, that's very dangerous.

RAMSEY CLARK

(FORMER ATTORNEY GENERAL OF THE UNITED STATES)

United States Army, he stood up to armies everywhere in support of the proposition that, "Unless you have a very good reason to kill, war is wrong."

"I don't think Ali was aware of the impact that his not going in the army would have on other people," says his longtime friend, Howard Bingham. "Ali was just doing what he thought was right for him. He had no idea at the time that this was going to affect how people all over the United States would react to the war and the draft."

Many Americans vehemently condemned Ali's stand. It came at a time when most people in the United States still supported the war. But as Julian Bond later observed, "When a figure as heroic and beloved as Muhammad Ali stood up and said, 'No, I won't go,' it reverberated through the whole society. When Ali refused to take the symbolic step forward, everybody knew about it moments later. You could hear people talking about it on street corners. It was on everyone's lips. People who had never thought about the war before began to think it through because of Ali. The ripples were enormous."

"The government didn't need Ali to fight the war," Ramsey Clark, then the Attorney General of the United States, recalls. "But they would have loved to put him in the service; get his picture in there; maybe give him a couple of stripes on his sleeve, and take him all over the world. Think of the power that would have had in Africa, Asia, and South America. Here's this proud American serviceman, fighting symbolically for his country. They would have loved to do that."

But instead, what the government got was a reaffirmation of Ali's earlier statement — "I ain't got no quarrel with them Vietcong." "And that rang serious alarm bells," says Noam Chomsky, "because it raised the question of why poor people in the United States were being forced by rich people in the United States to kill poor people in Vietnam. Putting it simply, that's what it amounted to. And Ali put it very simply in ways that people could understand."

Ali's refusal to accept induction placed him once and for all at the vortex of the sixties. "You had riots in the streets; you had assassinations; you had the war in Vietnam," Dave Kindred of the *Atlanta Journal-Constitution* remembers. "It was a violent, turbulent, almost indecipherable time in America, and Ali was in all of those fires at once, in addition to being heavyweight champion of the world."

That championship was soon taken from Ali, but he never wavered from his cause. Speaking to a college audience, he proclaimed, "I would like to say to those of you who think I've lost so much, I have gained everything. I have peace of heart; I have a clear, free conscience. And I'm proud. I wake up happy. I go to bed happy. And if I go to jail, I'll go to jail happy. Boys go to war and die for what they believe, so I don't see why the world is so shook up over me suffering for what I believe. What's so unusual about that?"

"It really impressed me that Ali gave up his title," says former heavyweight champion Larry Holmes, who understands the measure of Ali's sacrifice as well as anyone. "Once you have it, you never want to lose it; because once you lose it, it's hard to get it back." But by the late sixties, Ali was more than heavyweight champion. That had become almost a side issue. He was a living embodiment of the proposition that principles matter. And the most powerful thing about him was no longer his fists; it was his conscience and the composure with which he carried himself:

FACING PAGE: *Ali's refusal to accept induction into the United States Army placed him at the vortex of the sixties.*

- Kwame Toure (formerly known as Stokely Carmichael): *Muhammad Ali used himself as a perfect instrument to advance the struggle of humanity by demonstrating clearly that principles are more important than material wealth. It's not just what Ali did. The way he did it was just as important.*

- Wilbert McClure (Ali's roommate and fellow gold-medal winner at the Olympics): *He always carried himself with his head high and with grace and composure. And we can't say that about all of his detractors; some of them in political office, some of them in pulpits, some of them thought of as nice upstanding citizens. No, we can't say that about all of them.*

- Charles Morgan (former Director of the American Civil Liberties Union Southern Office): *I remember thinking at the time, what kind of a foolish world am I living in where people want to put this man in jail.*

- Dave Kindred: *He was one thing, always. He was always brave.*

Ali was far from perfect, and it would do him a disservice not to acknowledge his flaws. It's hard to imagine a person so powerful yet at times so naive — almost on the order of Forrest Gump. On occasion, Ali has acted irrationally. He cherishes honor and is an honorable person, but too often excuses dishonorable behavior in others. His accommodation with dictators like Mobutu Sese Seko and Ferdinand Marcos and his willingness to fight in their countries stands in stark contrast to his love of freedom. There is nothing redeeming in one black person calling another black person a "gorilla," which was the label that Ali affixed to Joe Frazier. Nor should one gloss over Ali's past belief in racial separatism and the profligate womanizing of his younger days. But the things that Ali has done right in his life far outweigh the mistakes of his past. And the rough edges of his earlier years have been long since forgiven or forgotten.

What remains is a legacy of monumental proportions and a living reminder of just how good people can be. Muhammad Ali's influence on an entire nation, black and white, and a whole world of nations has been incalculable. He's not just a champion. A champion is someone who wins an athletic competition. Ali goes beyond that.

It was inevitable that someone would come along and break the color barrier in major league baseball. Jackie Robinson did it in a glorious way that personified his own dignity and courage. But if Jackie Robinson hadn't been there, someone else — Roy Campanella, Willie Mays, Henry Aaron — would have stepped in with his own brand of excitement and grace and opened baseball's doors. With or without Jack Johnson, eventually a black man would have won the heavyweight championship of the world. And sooner or later, there would have been a black athlete who, like Joe Louis, was universally admired and loved. But Ali carved out a place in history that was, and remains, uniquely his own. And it's unlikely that anyone other than Muhammad Ali could have created and fulfilled that role. Ali didn't just mirror his times. He wasn't a passive figure carried along by currents stronger than he was. He fought the current; he swam against the tide. He stood for something, stayed with it, and prevailed.

Muhammad Ali is an international treasure. More than anyone else of his generation, he belongs to the people of the world and is loved by them. No matter what happens in the years ahead, he has already made us better. He encouraged millions of people to believe in themselves, raise their aspirations, and accomplish things that might not have been done without him. He wasn't just a standard-bearer for black Americans. He stood up for everyone.

And that's the importance of Muhammad Ali.

FACING PAGE: *February 25, 1964. The moment of victory. Clay has recognized what his cornermen Angelo Dundee (left) and Drew "Bundini" Brown have not: that Sonny Liston has quit on his stool, and Clay is the new heavyweight champion of the world.*

WE WERE IN ELEMENTARY SCHOOL TOGETHER, AND HE WAS JUST ANOTHER ONE OF THE KIDS. YOU PUSH AND YOU SHOVE EACH OTHER, AND GET INTO THE NORMAL FIGHTS. THERE WERE DAYS HE LOST, AND THERE WERE DAYS HE WON. SO WHEN HE BEAT SONNY LISTON TO WIN THE CHAMPIONSHIP, SOME OF US WERE LAUGHING ABOUT IT; SAYING, "HE'S NOT EVEN UNDEFEATED IN THE NEIGHBORHOOD. HOW CAN HE BE CHAMPION OF THE WORLD?"

JIM BELL
(A CHILDHOOD CLASSMATE OF CASSIUS CLAY)

If I wanted to teach a little grandchild of mine about the universe, I'd go and get Muhammad Ali's story and say, "Here is what happened to the universe. One day, something went from nothing to BOOMMMM. The big bang. And it keeps getting bigger."

DICK GREGORY

ABOVE: *Scenes from Cassius Clay's amateur career.* CLOCKWISE FROM TOP LEFT: *Training at Louisville's Columbia Gym; in 1959, with his first coach, Joe Martin, who is admiring Clay's Golden Glove pendant; attracting the media, even in the early days of his career; preparing for the Olympics in 1960.*

Top: *With brother Rudy, in 1962, outside the house they grew up in.*

Young Cassius Clay always wanted a pink convertible, just like the one Sugar Ray Robinson owned. And when h

I went down to Louisville to do a story about Ali in the late 1960s. Louisville was a Jim Crow city then, so when we went out to eat, we had to go to the black section of town. I was there for four or five days. Every night, we went to the same restaurant. It had an eight-ounce steak and a sixteen-ounce steak on the menu. Every night, he ordered a thirty-two-ounce steak, and every night they gave it to him. Finally, after two or three nights, I asked him, "How do you know they have a thirty-two-ounce steak? It's not on the menu." And he told me, "When I found out you were coming, I went in and told the people here to order them for me." But if there was a moment when I really totally fell in love with this kid, it was when we were driving down the main street in Louisville. We stopped for a traffic light, and there was a very pretty girl standing on the corner. A white girl. I turned to Cassius, which was his name then, and said, "Boy, she's pretty." And he grabbed me, and said, "You're crazy, man. You can get electrocuted for that; a Jew looking at a white girl in Kentucky."

DICK SCHAAP

LEFT: *July 20, 1962. Alejandro Lavorante felt Clay's power when he was knocked out in the fifth round.*
ABOVE: *Clay's early professional career was guided by The Louisville Sponsoring Group: eleven white men, most of whom were heirs to old-line Kentucky fortunes.*

He was a sophomore in high school. Somebody had to dust up the library. And a schoolmate, who had been doing the job and was going to leave, brought him over. He was already known. Unknown to me, but he was appearing in Golden Gloves tournaments at the time, and had a whole bag of trophies that he brought out to show me later when I found out that he was a boxing champion. His friend introduced him to me as Cassius Clay. I said, "Do they call you Cass?" And he told me, "No ma'am; Cassius Marcellus Clay, Junior." So I said, "Okay; it will be Cassius." And he was polite; he was gentle. He always appeared on time and related to his work beautifully. Except one time. His father was a painter. And Cassius was kind of given to art too, so I gave him a paint job down in the lower area where we

"DO THEY CALL YOU CASS?"

were working. And he resisted. He used enamel where I had asked him to use flat paint. I said, "I thought your father was a painter." And he told me that his father was an artist, not a barn painter. And he just lived boxing. He worked at it very hard. One evening — he'd been training pretty heavily I think — I came back from dinner. And we had some reading tables in the stacks on the second floor. I looked in, and there was Cassius on one of the tables, asleep, facing the wall. I said, "Cassius, are you sick?" He raised himself up, kind of stunned because he'd fallen into a deep sleep, and told me, no. And after he became famous — you read about places where they say, "Abraham Lincoln slept here" — well, I take people into the stacks and I tell them, "Cassius Clay slept here."

- - - - - - - - - - -

SISTER J. ELLEN HUFF
(WHO SUPERVISED CASSIUS CLAY'S FIRST REGULAR AFTER-SCHOOL JOB)

FACING PAGE: *The mirror might have been Cassius Clay's favorite piece of gym equipment.*

I've never considered myself an expert on sports. No matter what the sport is, I never played any of those games well enough to consider myself an expert. But I do consider myself an expert on people. And there was something about Ali that made him a champion from the time he was a kid.

Dick Schaap

ABOVE AND FACING PAGE: *Early in his career, Clay trained under Angelo Dundee's tutelage at Miami's legendary Fifth Street Gym.*

God's got me here for something. I can feel it. I was born for everything that I'm doing now.

MUHAMMAD ALI

FOLLOWING PAGES: *Even before Clay was a world champion, his sparring sessions attracted a crowd.*

Ali could convince you that his ice cube was colder. I mean, if he had an ice cube and you had

one, his ice cube was colder than your ice cube.

- - - - - - - - - -

BUTCH LEWIS

(ONCE JOE FRAZIER'S "ROAD BUDDY")

ABOVE AND FACING PAGE: *To gain valuable national exposure in* Life *magazine in 1961. Cassius Clay tricked a photographer into thinking he trained underwater.*

My wife Jean and I and Jesse Jackson were over at Joe Louis's house, because Jesse had some business with Joe's wife. Jean, Jesse, and I were sitting with Mrs. Louis in the dining room, having some fried chicken, which was absolutely delicious. Joe was in the bedroom, laying in bed, looking at television. Then he came to the door, and said, "Cassius is on TV; Cassius is on TV." So we all got up to see Ali on TV. He was being interviewed, and he was saying, "I'm not an Uncle Tom like Joe Louis." He kept on ranting and calling Joe Louis an Uncle Tom, and I'm standing there with Joe Louis. I don't know how on earth it happened that I got into that position. The Lord just put me there, I guess. Joe didn't say anything. He just went on back to bed. But the next time I saw Ali, I made a point of telling him, "I can't stand to have the hero of my adulthood talking like that about the hero of my childhood. Joe Louis meant so much to us. No matter what you think, you have no right to say those things about him. You don't know what you're talking about. You don't know what conditions Joe Louis came up under. If it hadn't been for Joe Louis, you wouldn't be here." And I think, after a while, Ali understood that.

OSCAR BROWN, JR.

(WHO LATER WROTE THE MUSIC FOR *BUCK WHITE*, THE BROADWAY SHOW THAT ALI STARRED IN DURING HIS EXILE FROM BOXING)

•

ABOVE: *Cassius Clay, in 1962, with Sugar Ray Robinson and Joe Louis. "This is my favorite picture of me ever," Ali said later, "because I was young and I was with my heroes."*
FACING PAGE: *After some early hard feelings between them, Ali and Joe Louis were friends at the end.*

Ali and Joe Louis had harsh words for each other. They had different beliefs about religion. They had different beliefs about patriotism. But I think what really bugged Ali about Joe Louis was that Louis never gave Ali credit for being a great fighter. And Joe Louis was a great fighter himself, so he had to know how truly great Ali was.

JOSE TORRES

There were some hard feelings early on, but Ali and Joe Louis got to be friendly later. And there was one thing I've never figured out. When Ali saw Joe Louis, he'd start dancing and boxing, throwing punches real close to Joe's face, right in his face. "I'll eat you up; you're too slow; come on, Joe." Every time, he'd do that. Joe would move back, like he didn't want to be bothered, and Ali would keep it up; dancing around him, throwing punches real fast. It never failed. And all of a sudden, Joe Louis would reach out and slap Ali right upside the face. Bop! A left hand, real quick. That would end it. And I never figured out whether Ali allowed it to happen that way or he couldn't stop it. Because, you see, Ali was a humanitarian, and he got a kick out of making you be who you were, and making you better than you were supposed to be. So I don't know if he let Joe Louis slap him or not.

PAT PATTERSON
(THE CHICAGO POLICEMAN WHO SERVED ALI AS A SECURITY AIDE)

Brother Cassius will never do anything that will in any way tarnish or take away from his image as the heavyweight champion of the world. He is trying his best to live a clean life and project a clean image. But despite this, you will find that the press is constantly trying to paint him as something other than what he actually is. He doesn't smoke. He doesn't drink. He's never been involved in any trouble. His record is clean. If he was white, they'd be referring to him as the all-American boy.

- - - - - - - - - -

MALCOLM X

ABOVE: *Malcolm X diligently recorded Cassius Clay's growing popularity.*

I'd like to see peace on Earth. If separation will bring it, I say let's separate. If integrating will bring it, I say let's integrate. But let's not just stand still with one man holding another in bondage and depriving him of freedom, justice, and equality, neither integrating or letting him go to self.

- - - - - - - - - -

MUHAMMAD ALI

40

Ali's treatment of women when he was young isn't something that should be emulated. But the things he did right were more important than the things he did wrong. He made black women feel good about being black, the same way he made black men feel good about themselves. He made black women feel every bit as beautiful and desirable as white women.

TOM HOOVER

(A FRIEND)

ABOVE: *Surrounded by fans in Louisville, 1963.*

I learned a lot from him. I learned about laughing and enjoying and having fun with your work. I learned that life doesn't have to be solemn to be serious. He never believed all the myths and legends. He understood that a lot of it was show, and he would wink and let you know. He taught me that you can do so much with a wink. The athletes, the politicians, the people who don't wink; they're the ones who should frighten you.

DICK SCHAAP

ABOVE: *February 1964. While training in Miami Beach to challenge Sonny Liston, Clay met with the Beatles shortly after the "Fab Four's" first appearance on* The Ed Sullivan Show.

Muhammad was always susceptible to the left hook; against Sonny Banks, against Henry Cooper, against Joe Frazier, whoever.

You see, no matter how great a fighter is, he always has flaws. And Muhammad's problem was that left hook. He always had a

problem evading it.

ANGELO DUNDEE

THE BUILD-UP TO CASSIUS CLAY VERSUS SONNY LISTON
FACING PAGE.TOP: *Clay was brave with Liston in hand, but few observers thought he'd be able to deal with the real thing.*
BOTTOM: *Clay, shown sharing a reflective moment with his mother, actively promoted the bout.*
ABOVE: *Liston (wearing a white cap) was unimpressed by Clay's pre-bout sparring sessions.*

Cassius Clay asked my husband if he would bring our whole family down [to Miami Beach for the first

Liston fight]. It was supposed to be our anniversary present. I was expecting, so my husband had to do

some prodding to get me on a plane and to get our three little girls ready, but of course we went. And

Cassius was a nervous wreck. He had a great deal of apprehension about fighting Sonny Liston. But my

BROTHER MUHAMMAD

husband talked to him like a little brother and helped him conquer his fear. And this was after Malcolm had

been cautioned not to go. He was told by Elijah Muhammad that, if he went, it would be on his own as an

individual, not representing the Nation of Islam; and that, if he had good sense, he would stay away,

because there was no way Cassius Clay could win. But Malcolm felt that, if Cassius Clay was totally focused

on the fight, he could win. And one of the things he said to me was, "If he loses, he should not be alone."

DR. BETTY SHABAZZ
(WIDOW OF MALCOLM X)

FACING PAGE: *Malcolm X was a significant presence in Cassius Clay's camp in the days leading up to the first Liston bout.*
FOLLOWING PAGES: *In their first bout, showing uncanny reflexes and timing, Clay repeatedly leaned away from Sonny Liston's jab.*

Ali is the only person I've ever seen who I knew was protected. Against all odds, he always came up with something because he's a spiritual person, and I don't necessarily mean religion. One thing I know for sure — you can't use logic when you talk about Muhammad Ali.

JIM BROWN
(FORMER FOOTBALL GREAT AND FOUNDER OF THE BLACK ECONOMIC UNION)

ABOVE: *February 25, 1964: Liston found that there was no escaping Clay's jab and fast right hand.*
FACING PAGE: *Moments after Liston quit, bedlam erupted in the new champion's corner, as Bundini Brown and Angelo Dundee rushed to embrace him.*

This is a man who spent his whole life telling the world, "I Am The Greatest!" And whenever you got exasperated with him and said, "Shut up, because you're not," he'd do something to prove that he was.

- - - - - - - - - -

JERRY IZENBERG

A lot of people were afraid because he changed his name. You can't change your name. It's an awful thing to do to change your name.

You don't believe that? Ask Coca-Cola. Tell them to change their name.

DICK GREGORY
(POLITICAL ACTIVIST AND HUMAN RIGHTS ADVOCATE)

FACING PAGE: *Ali showed almost reverential respect for Nation of Islam leader Elijah Muhammad.*
ABOVE: *Before his conversion to Orthodox Islam, Ali was a huge drawing card at Nation of Islam rallies.*

Africa was very interesting for Ali and myself. We went over there for the first time in 1964. And we'd heard things about Africa — Tarzan, and everybody's in huts; stuff like that. We landed at the airport, and the first thing we saw was Mobil Oil signs, Coca-Cola, and this and that. And Ali said, "Hey, the white man is here too."

HOWARD BINGHAM

•

LEFT: *In May 1964, the newly crowned champion embarked on a tour of Africa that included a relaxed moment on the Nile River in Egypt with Herbert Muhammad, the son of Elijah Muhammad, who would become Ali's manager in 1966.*
ABOVE: *Ali married his first wife, Sonji Roi, in August 1964 after a six-week courtship.*

My outlook on life is really the same as 90 percent of the white people in America. They're just shocked and surprised that we who follow the teachings of Elijah Muhammad want to be with ourselves and don't want to integrate. That's a surprise to whites, which makes us controversial and different. But really, we're not different. We're just different from the Negro who's striving for forced integration. But as a whole, whites believe the same thing we do and have been believing it for all time.

- - - - - - - - - -

MUHAMMAD ALI

ABOVE: *Like their male counterparts, women in the Nation of Islam viewed Ali with pride.*

I'm an easy target. I'm everywhere; everybody knows me. I walk the streets daily, and nobody's guarding me. I have no guns, no police. So if someone's gonna get me, tell them to come on and get it over with — if they can get past God, because God is controlling the bullet.

MUHAMMAD ALI

ABOVE: *Ali's jab, the way it must have looked to his ring opponents.*

Even though he's still with us, I miss him. I miss his voice. I miss his sense of the absurd. Ali had a sense of the

unpredictability and craziness and hypocrisy of life. And I wish he was still running around, making speeches and

doing all the other things he used to do. You know, in addition to being the quintessential civil disobedient and a

walking lesson in decency and independence, Ali was one of the few people I know of who could make almost

anyone laugh out loud.

- - - - - - - - - - -

WILLIAM NACK

(WRITER FOR SPORTS ILLUSTRATED)

FACING PAGE: *Threatening to "collar that big ugly bear," Ali taunted Liston before their rematch.*
ABOVE LEFT: *Ali's histrionics continued as the second Liston fight drew near.*
ABOVE RIGHT: *Ali's charisma opened many doors, as shown in this 1964 recording session. His favorite song? "Stand By Me."*

Muhammad Ali rates his opponents:

*   **The scariest — Sonny Liston**

*   **The most skilled as a boxer — Floyd Patterson**

*   **The most powerful — George Foreman**

*   **The roughest and toughest — Joe Frazier**

- - - - - - - - - -

Muhammad Ali rates the greatest heavyweights of all time:

(1) Me

(2) Jack Johnson

(3) Joe Louis

- - - - - - - - - -

Muhammad Ali's list of "The Ten Best-Looking Heavyweight

Champions Ever"

I'm number one. After me, it don't matter.

- - - - - - - - - -

●

LEFT: *A confident Muhammad Ali watched Sonny Liston weigh in just prior to their return bout.*

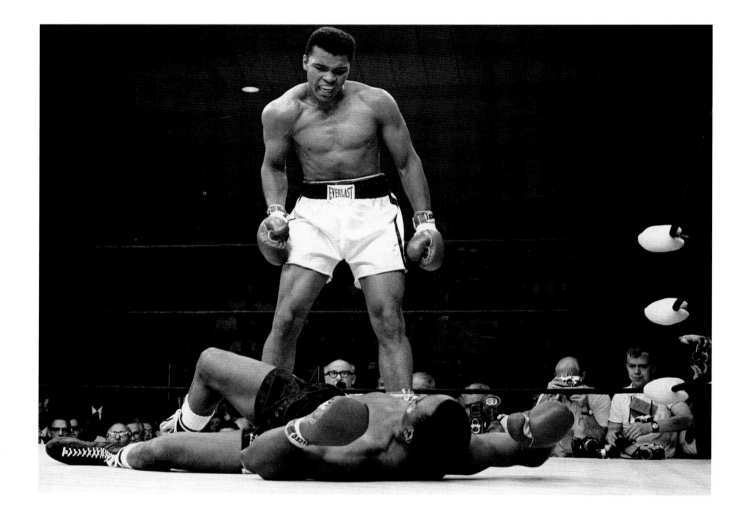

I feel the greatest prize in sports is the heavyweight championship of the world. I happen to have been successful in baseball, but if you want to talk about dedication, take a fighter who climbs to the top and stays there for as long as Ali. He was absolutely devoted to being the best, and he was one of the greatest fighters who ever lived. I've seen him fight live; I've seen all his films. And what always amazes me is the way he maneuvered in the ring. There's no question in my mind that he was the fastest big man ever in boxing. And I think he got as much out of his physical ability as possible, which is another reason I admire him. He came as close as any athlete I know to getting the most out of his potential.

- - - - - - - - - - -

TED WILLIAMS

•

ABOVE AND FACING PAGE: *May 25, 1965: Ali stands over a fallen Sonny Liston in the first round of their championship rematch, and moments later raises his arm in triumph.*

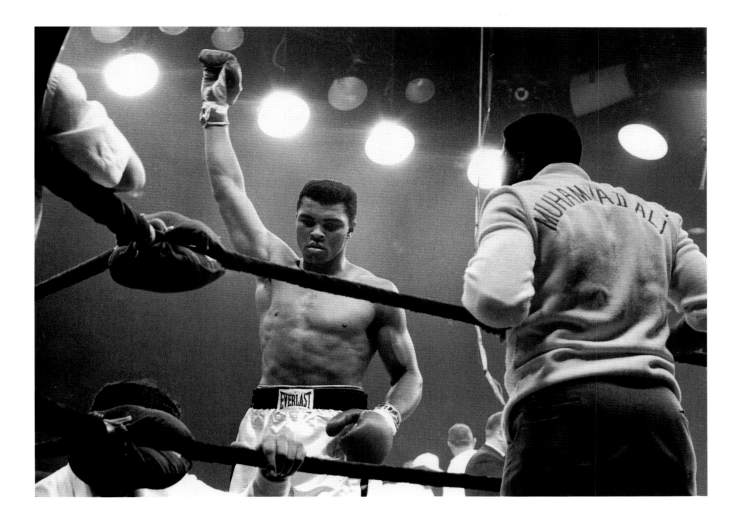

I didn't pay much attention to the religious stuff and the Vietnam stuff. I just watched what Ali did in the ring, and he was great. I guess what impressed me most about Ali was the way he stayed number one for so long. Somebody came out with a book once about the best baseball players in history. I was number sixteen or seventeen, which isn't bad, but it's not like being number one. And you can argue about who was the greatest fighter of all time, but Ali was the best when he was in his prime. He was on top during his career, and that's something I could never really say. I always figured Willie Mays was better than me. All you had to do was look at the statistics, and Willie came out better than me. There were years like 1956 and 1961 when I did better than Willie, but over the long run he did better than me. So I can't really say that I was number one. Ali can. He was "The Greatest."

MICKEY MANTLE

All his fights worried me. I was always happy when the final bell had rung, and it was like, phew, it's over. Even the easy fights were hard for me.

HOWARD BINGHAM

ABOVE: *Ali had little trouble knocking out Floyd Patterson in their 1965 bout.*

FACING PAGE: *George Churalo went the distance against Ali in 1966, but couldn't cope with the champion's speed.*

FOLLOWING PAGES: *Ali took London by storm when he arrived for his 1966 rematch against Henry Cooper.*

My intention is never to hurt an opponent. I don't actually carry fights in a way that's crooked, but I will admit that I've seen opponents in physical unconsciousness on their feet and saw chances to really hurt them to the extent where it was possible to have a brain concussion, and I knew I was winning, and the fight was just about over, so I backed off. Henry Cooper was an example. He bleeds easy. Whenever he gets cut, blood gushes. And as soon as I saw that, I lost all my fighting instinct and backed off, hoping the referee would stop it. I don't like really hurting someone for the pleasure of a bloodthirsty audience. These other people in other sports, they're out to kill each other. Professional football players go out on the field to hurt somebody. But not me; I'm a classy boxer. I don't want to kill nobody. I'm out there to box. All I want to do is make points.

MUHAMMAD ALI

FACING PAGE: *As he readied to fight Henry Cooper, Ali's every move in training was watched by the British public.*
ABOVE: *Ali's victory, and Cooper's defeat, were all but inevitable. And once again, England mourned.*

Ali: I wanted to make him big, but not that big. I created a Frankenstein monster.

Howard Cosell: It's like the song from "My Fair Lady." I've grown accustomed to his face. He almost makes my day begin. I love him.

The only bad thing that Ali left behind was his boxing style. His style — hands down, chin up in the air — is detrimental to fighters who try to imitate him, because they don't have the timing, the genius, and the magic that Ali had. So they try to imitate him, and they get knocked out.

JOSE TORRES

ABOVE: *On November 14, 1966, Ali put Cleveland Williams on the canvas four times en route to a decisive third-round knockout.*
FACING PAGE: *On February 6, 1967, Ali taunted and battered Ernie Terrell for fifteen rounds to win a lopsided unanimous decision.*

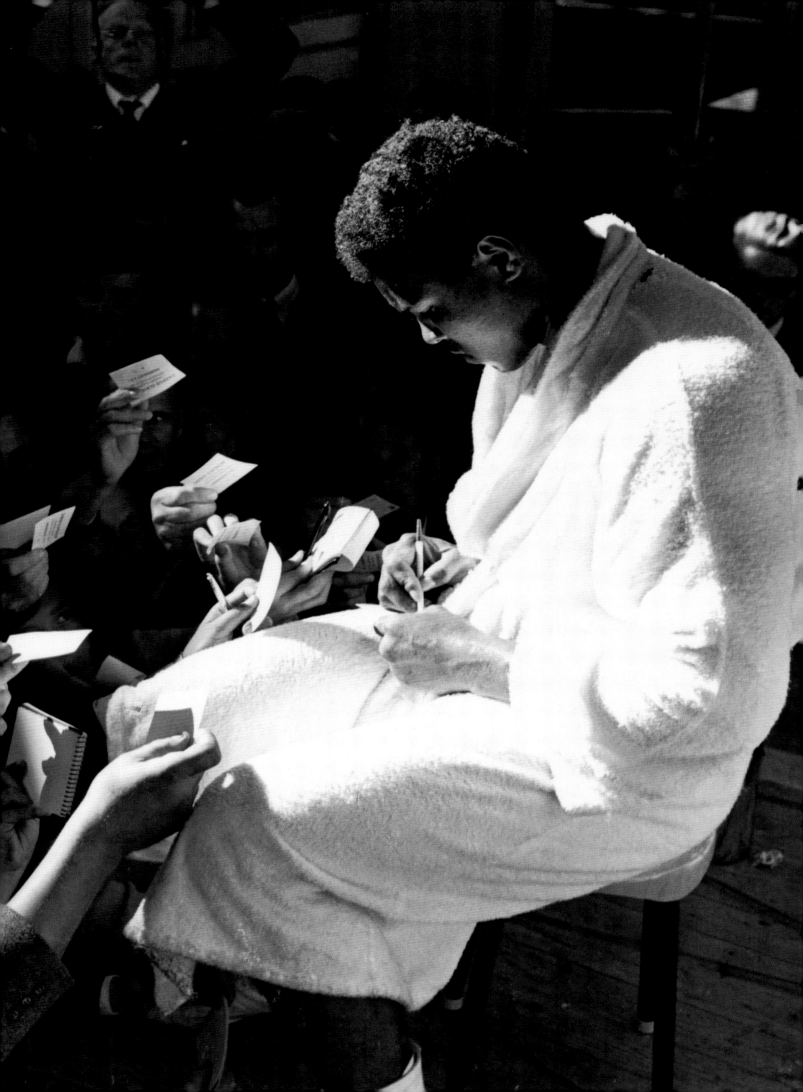

Going to jail was my job. I'd been arrested twenty-five times in Mississippi and Alabama. So when they

told me, "We'll send you to jail for five years," what I did was, I sat down and worked out a list of books

that I'd finally get a chance to read. I wasn't worried. I'd get a chance to sleep; no telephones. I'm used to jail.

I wasn't giving up anything. But Muhammad Ali had everything. Fame, glory, money, women, good looks,

champion of the world. So when Muhammad would call me — we'd speak back and forth on the telephone

— and he'd tell me, "I ain't going," I'd say, "Yeah; right on!" But I always wondered, when that final moment

comes and he actually has to take that step, how will it come out? Because, no question, the FBI viewed

Ali as more of a threat than H. Rap Brown and myself. Muhammad Ali had a broader base than we had.

"GOING TO JAIL WAS MY JOB"

The government recognized that Muhammad Ali could cause more trouble than all of us. That's why we

understood that the weight of the blow would be hardest against Muhammad Ali. They were going to take his

championship crown; no doubt about it. They were going to prosecute him; no doubt about it. They were going

to do everything possible to bring him to his knees. And of all the people who opposed the war in Vietnam,

I think that Muhammad Ali risked the most. Lots of people refused to go. Some went to jail. But no one

risked as much from their decision not to go to war in Vietnam as Muhammad Ali. And his real greatness

can be seen in the fact that, despite all that was done to him, he became even greater and more humane.

- - - - - - - - - -

KWAME TOURE
(FORMERLY KNOWN AS STOKELY CARMICHAEL)

•

FACING PAGE: *As 1967 progressed, Ali knew that he would soon be forced to relinquish his crown.*

Reporter: Why won't you fight for your country?

Ali: I'm a minister of my religion, and this country has
    laws for ministers. George Hamilton; why don't he
    fight for his country? He's making a movie. Joe
    Namath; why don't he fight for his country? He's
    playing football.

Reporter: Joe Namath has a bad knee.

Ali: Yeah; ain't that silly. I saw Joe Namath playing
    football the other day. Twenty-seven passes out of
    forty-three is all he hit. Go talk to him about fighting
    for his country. I'm not using them as excuses, but
    you all keep jumping on me like I'm the last one;
    like you'll lose the war if I ain't in it.

- - - - - - - - - - -

He's hurting the morale of a lot of young Negro soldiers
over in Vietnam. And the tragedy to me is, Cassius has
made millions of dollars off of the American public, and
now he's not willing to show his appreciation to a country
that's giving him, in my view, a fantastic opportunity.
That hurts a great number of people.

- - - - - - - - - - -

JACKIE ROBINSON, 1967

ABOVE AND RIGHT: *Ali spoke his mind, and then was
surrounded by the media after refusing induction into
the United States Army.*
FOLLOWING PAGES: *Although Ali was stripped of his title
and banned from boxing, his popularity among the
masses was continuing to grow.*

We were taught when we were little children that Mary had a little lamb, its fleece was white as snow. Then we heard about Snow White. White Owl cigars. White Swan soap. White Cloud tissue. White Rain hair rinse. White Tornado floor wax. White Plus toothpaste. All the good cowboys ride white horses and wear white hats. The President lives in the White House. Jesus was white. The Last Supper was white. The angels is white. Miss America is white. Even Tarzan, the King of the Jungle in Africa, is white.

MUHAMMAD ALI, 1967

ABOVE: *During his exile from boxing, Ali lectured frequently on college campuses.*

When a man's guilty, you don't just say, you're guilty. You hold court and prove it, and then you say he's guilty. You don't tell a

man he murdered somebody without giving him a chance to explain and without letting the world see why you're condemning

him. I never heard of them taking nobody else's title. People such as Sonny Liston have been in jail fifteen or twenty times. There's

people with scandals, people who've been caught in their cars, breaking speed limits and carrying guns. And they don't get

suspended, so what's the reason for suspending me?

MUHAMMAD ALI

ABOVE: *In June 1967, a group of prominent black athletes met with Ali to discuss his future. Among them were* (first row)
Bill Russell, Jim Brown, and Lew Alcindor (who would later change his name to Kareem Abdul-Jabbar).

It's very difficult to explain to young people today how important Ali was, because the society has changed so much over the past thirty years. Now black pride is taken for granted. People understand that it's possible to be a patriotic American, and still believe that the war in Vietnam was wrong. And everything today is driven by money; particularly in sports, where athletes think they're making a sacrifice if they can't wear clothes with their favorite logo on them at an Olympic awards ceremony. I mean, how do you explain to a twelve-year-old that Muhammad Ali, based on an act of principle, risked going to jail and sacrificed the heavyweight championship of the world. Try explaining that to a young person today. He'll look at you like you're crazy; or maybe he'll think it was Ali who was crazy.

– – – – – – – – – – –

WALLY MATTHEWS
(BOXING WRITER FOR THE *NEW YORK POST*)

What do you mean, project a good image? An image to who? Who don't like the image I project? That's the weakest thing I've heard yet; I'm not a good image. For my people, I'm the best image in the world.

– – – – – – – – – – –

MUHAMMAD ALI

ABOVE AND FOLLOWING PAGES: *Ali has always been drawn to people, be it on the streets of Chicago or in the classroom.*

PART TWO

MUHAMMAD ALI AND BOXING

"You could spend twenty years studying Ali," Dave Kindred once wrote, "and still not know what

he is or who he is. He's a wise man, and he's a child. I've never seen anyone who was so giving and, at the

same time, so self-centered. He's either the most complex guy that I've ever been around or the most

simple. And I still can't figure out which it is. I mean, I truly don't know. We were sure who Ali was only

when he danced before us in the dazzle of the ring lights. Then he could hide nothing."

And so it was that the world first came to know Muhammad Ali, not as a person, not as a social,

political, or religious figure, but as a fighter.

FACING PAGE AND ABOVE: *Whether hitting the speed bag as Cassius Clay in 1963 (above) or resting after a sparring session in 1972,*
Ali's good looks belied the fact that, beneath his sweet exterior, there was a tough man at work.

His early professional bouts infuriated and entertained as much as they impressed. Cassius Clay held his hands too low. He backed away from punches, rather than bobbing and weaving out of danger, and lacked true knockout power. Purists cringed when he predicted the round in which he intended to knock out his opponent, and grimaced when he did so and bragged about each new conquest.

Then, at age twenty-two, Clay challenged Sonny Liston for the world heavyweight crown. Liston was widely regarded as the most intimidating, ferocious, powerful fighter of his era. Clay was such a prohibitive underdog that Robert Lipsyte, who covered the bout for the *New York Times*, was instructed to "find out the directions from the arena to the nearest hospital, so I wouldn't waste deadline time getting there after Clay was knocked out." But as David Ben-Gurion once proclaimed, "Anyone who doesn't believe in miracles is not a realist." Cassius Clay knocked out Sonny Liston to become heavyweight champion of the world.

Officially, Ali's reign as champion was divided into three segments. And while he fought through the administrations of seven presidents, his greatness as a fighter was most clearly on display in the three years after he first won the crown. During the course of thirty-seven months, Ali fought ten times. No heavyweight in history has defended his title more frequently against more formidable opposition in more dominant fashion than Ali did in those years.

Boxing, in the first instance, is about not getting hit. "And I can't be hit," Ali told the world. "It's impossible for me to lose, because there's not a man on earth with the speed and ability to beat me." In his rematch with Liston, which ended in a first-round knockout, Ali was hit only twice. Victories over Floyd Patterson, George Chuvalo, Henry Cooper, Brian London, and Karl Mildenberger followed. Then, on November 14, 1966, Ali did battle against Cleveland Williams. Over the course of three rounds, Ali landed more than one hundred punches, scored four knockdowns, and was hit a total of three times. "The hypocrites and phonies are all shook up because everything I said would come true did come true," Ali chortled afterward. "I said I was The Greatest, and they thought I was just acting the fool. Now, instead of admitting that I'm the best heavyweight in all history, they don't know what to do."

Ali's triumph over Cleveland Williams was followed by victories over Ernie Terrell and Zora Folley. Then, after refusing induction into the United States Army, he was stripped of his title and forced out of boxing. "If I never fight again, this is the last of the champions," Ali said of his, and boxing's, plight. "The next title is a political belt, a racial belt, an organization belt. There's no more real world champion until I'm physically beat."

In October 1970, Ali was allowed to return to boxing, but his skills were no longer the same. The legs that had allowed him to "dance" for fifteen rounds without stopping no longer carried him as surely around the ring. His reflexes, while still superb, were no longer lightning fast. Ali prevailed in his first two comeback fights, against Jerry Quarry and Oscar Bonavena. Then he challenged Joe Frazier, who was the "organization" champion by virtue of victories over Buster Mathis and Jimmy Ellis.

"Champion of the world? Ain't but one champion," Ali said before his first bout against Frazier. "How you gonna have two champions of the world? He's an alternate champion. The real champion is back now." But Frazier thought otherwise. And on March 8, 1971, he bested Ali over fifteen brutal rounds. "He's not a great boxer," Ali said afterward. "But he's a great slugger, a great street fighter, a bull fighter. He takes a lot of punches, his eyes close, and he just keeps coming. I figured he could take the punches. But one thing surprised me in this fight, and that's that he landed his left hook as regular as he did. Usually, I don't get hit over and over with the same punch, and he hit me solid a lot of times."

FACING PAGE: *Ali was an unwelcome guest at Joe Frazier's training camp in Philadelphia prior to their first fight.*

Some fighters can't handle defeat. They fly so high when they're on top, that a loss brings them irrevocably crashing down. "What was interesting to me after the loss to Frazier," says Ferdie Pacheco, "was we'd seen this undefeatable guy; now how was he going to handle defeat? Was he going to be a cry baby? Was he going to be crushed? Well, what we found out was, this guy takes defeat like he takes victory. All he said was, I'll beat him next time."

What Ali said was plain and simple: "I got to whup Joe Frazier, because he beat me. Anybody would like to say, 'I retired undefeated.' I can't say that no more. But if I could say, 'I got beat, but I came back and beat him,' I'd feel better."

Following his loss to Frazier, Ali won ten fights in a row, eight of them against world-class opponents. Then, in March 1973, he stumbled, when a little-known fighter named Ken Norton broke his jaw in the second round en route to a twelve-round upset decision. "I knew something was strange," Ali said after the bout, "because, if a bone is broken, the whole internalness in your body, everything, is nauseating. I didn't know what it was, but I could feel my teeth moving around, and I had to hold my teeth extra tight to keep the bottom from moving. My trainers wanted me to stop. But I was thinking about those nineteen thousand people in the arena, and *Wide World of Sports*, millions of people at home watching in sixty-two countries. So what I had to do was put up a good fight, go the distance, and not get hit on the jaw again."

Now Ali had a new target — a priority ahead of even Joe Frazier. "After Ali got his jaw broke, he wanted Norton bad," recalls Lloyd Wells, a longtime Ali confidante. "Herbert Muhammad [Ali's manager] was trying to put him in another fight, and Ali kept saying, 'No, get me Norton. I want Norton.' Herbert was saying, but we got a big purse; we got this, and we got that. And Ali was saying, 'No, just get me Norton. I don't want nobody but Norton.' "

Ali got Norton — and beat him. Then, after an interim bout against Rudi Lubbers, he got Joe Frazier again — and beat him too. From a technical point of view, the second Ali-Frazier bout was probably Ali's best performance after his exile from boxing. He did what he wanted to do, showing flashes of what he'd once been as a fighter but never would be again. Then Ali journeyed to Zaire to challenge George Foreman, who had dethroned Frazier to become heavyweight champion of the world.

"Foreman can punch but he can't fight," Ali said of his next foe. But most observers thought that Foreman could do both. As was the case when Ali fought Sonny Liston, he entered the ring a heavy underdog. Still, studying his opponent's armor, Ali thought he detected a flaw. Foreman's punching power was awesome, but his stamina and will were suspect. Thus, the "rope-a-dope" was born.

"The strategy on Ali's part was to cover up, because George was like a tornado," former boxing great Archie Moore, who was one of Foreman's cornermen that night, recalls. "And when you see a tornado coming, you run into the house and you cover up. You go into the basement and get out of the way of that strong wind, because you know that otherwise it's going to blow you away. That's what Ali did. He covered up and the storm was raging, but after a while, the storm blew itself out." Or phrased differently, "Yeah; Ali let Foreman punch himself out," says Jerry Izenberg. "But the rope-a-dope wouldn't have worked against Foreman for anyone in the world except Ali, because on top of everything else, Ali was tougher than everyone else. No one in the world except Ali could have taken George Foreman's punches."

Ali stopped Foreman in the eighth round to regain the heavyweight championship. Then, over the next thirty months, at the peak of his popularity as champion, he fought nine times. Those bouts showed Ali to be a courageous fighter, but a fighter on the decline. Like most aging combatants, he did his best to put

FACING PAGE: *October 30, 1974: George Foreman succumbed to the Ali magic, and a crushing right hand, in Zaire.*

Muhammad Ali rates his fights:

- When I was at my best — against Cleveland Williams

- The best fight for fans — against Joe Frazier in Manila

- The fight that meant the most to me — beating George Foreman to win the championship of the world again

We can all look back and say, "Well, Ali might have fought too long, or he might have got hit too many times. But it's hard to

ive boxing up when you've been doing it for a long time, and you know you were good, and you know you can still whup some

f the guys that's out there, but you just can't beat guys that's on a certain level. It was his decision, you know. He knew wha

oxing was all about, and he knew what he wanted to do. He made his life what it was. And I got to give the man credit. He

a positive spin on things. But viewed in realistic terms, "I'm more experienced" translated into "I'm getting older." "I'm stronger at this weight" meant "I should lose a few pounds." And "I'm more patient now" was a cover for "I'm slower." Eight of Ali's first nine fights during his second reign as champion did little to enhance his legacy. But sandwiched in between matches against the likes of Jean-Pierre Coopman and Richard Dunn and mediocre showings against more legitimate adversaries, Ali won what might have been the greatest fight of all time.

On October 1, 1975, Ali and Joe Frazier met in the Philippines, six miles outside of Manila, to do battle for the third time. "You have to understand the premise behind that fight," Ferdie Pacheco recalls. "The first fight was life and death, and Frazier won. Second fight: Ali figures him out; no problem, relatively easy victory for Ali. Then Ali beats Foreman, and Frazier's sun sets. And I don't care what anyone says now; all of us thought that Joe Frazier was shot. We all thought that this was going to be an easy fight. Ali comes out, dances around, and knocks him out in eight or nine rounds. That's what we figured. And you know what happened in that fight. Ali took a beating like you'd never believe anyone could take. When he said afterward that it was the closest thing he'd ever known to death — let me tell you something; if dying is that hard, I'd hate to see it coming. But Frazier took the same beating. And in the fourteenth round, Ali just about took his head off. I was cringing. The heat was awesome; both men were dehydrated; the place was like a time-bomb. I thought we were close to a fatality. It was a terrible moment, and then Frazier's corner stopped it."

"Ali-Frazier III was Ali-Frazier III," says Jerry Izenberg. "There's nothing to compare it with. I've never witnessed anything like it. And I'll tell you something — both fighters won that night, and both fighters lost."

Boxing is a tough business. The nature of the game is that fighters get hit. Ali himself inflicted a lot of damage on ring opponents during the course of his career. And in return: "I've been hit a lot," he acknowledged, one month before the third Frazier fight. "I take punishment every day in training. I take punishment in my fights. I take a lot of punishment; I just don't show it."

Still, as Ferdie Pacheco notes, "The human brain wasn't meant to get hit by a heavyweight punch. And the older you get, the more susceptible you are to damage. When are you best? Between fifteen and thirty. At that age, you're growing, you're strong, you're developing. You can take punches and come back. But inevitably, if you keep fighting, you reach an age when every punch can cause damage. Nature begins giving you little bills and the amount keeps escalating, like when you owe money to the IRS and the government keeps adding and compounding the damage."

In Manila, Joe Frazier landed 440 punches, many of those to Ali's head. After Manila would have been a good time for Ali to stop boxing, but too many people had a vested interest in his continuing to fight. Harold Conrad served for years as a publicist for Ali's bouts. "You get a valuable piece of property like Ali," Conrad said shortly before his death. "How are you going to put it out of business? It's like shutting down a factory or closing down a big successful corporation. The people who are making money off the workers just don't want to do it."

Thus, Ali fought on. In 1977, he was hurt badly but came back to win a close decision over Earnie Shavers. "In the second round, I had him in trouble," Shavers remembers. "I threw a right hand over Ali's jab, and I hurt him. He kind of wobbled. But Ali was so cunning, I didn't know if he was hurt or playing fox. I found out later that he was hurt; but he waved me in, so I took my time to be careful. I didn't want to go for the kill and get killed. And Ali was the kind of guy who, when you thought you had him hurt, he always seemed to come back. The guy seemed to pull off a miracle each time. I hit him a couple of good shots, but

89

FACING PAGE: *Joe Frazier moved relentlessly forward in Ali-Frazier III, the "Thrilla in Manila."*

he recovered better than any other fighter I've known."

Next up for Ali was Leon Spinks, a novice with an Olympic gold medal but only seven professional fights. "Spinks was in awe of Ali," Ron Borges of the *Boston Globe* recalls. "The day before their first fight, I was having lunch in the coffee shop at Caesar's Palace with Leon and [his trainer] Sam Solomon. No one knew who Leon was. Then Ali walked in, and everyone went crazy. 'Look; there's Ali! Omigod; it's him!' And Leon was like everybody else. He got all excited. He was shouting, 'Look; there he is! There's Ali!' In twenty-four hours, they'd be fighting each other, but right then, Leon was ready to carry Ali around the room on his shoulders."

The next night, Spinks captured Ali's title with a relentless fifteen-round assault. Seven months later, Ali returned the favor, regaining the championship with a fifteen-round victory of his own. Then he retired from boxing, but two years later made an ill-advised comeback against Larry Holmes.

"Before the Holmes fight, you could clearly see the beginnings of Ali's physical deterioration," remembers Barry Frank, who was representing Ali in various commercial endeavors on behalf of IMG. "The huskiness had already come into his voice, and he had a little bit of a balance problem. Sometimes he'd get up off a chair and, not stagger, but maybe take a half step to get his balance."

Realistically speaking, it was obvious that Ali had no chance of beating Larry Holmes. But there was always that kernel of doubt — would beating Holmes be any more extraordinary than knocking out Sonny Liston and George Foreman? Ali himself fanned the flames. "I'm so happy going into this fight," he said shortly before the bout. "I'm dedicating this fight to all the people who've been told, you can't do it. People who drop out of school because they're told they're dumb. People who go to crime because they don't think they can find jobs. I'm dedicating this fight to all of you people who have a Larry Holmes in your life. I'm gonna whup my Holmes, and I want you to whup your Holmes."

But Holmes put it more succinctly: "Ali is thirty-eight years old. His mind is making a date that his body can't keep."

Holmes was right. It was a horrible night. Old and seriously debilitated from the effects of an improperly prescribed drug called Thyrolar, Ali was a shell of his former self. He had no reflexes, no legs, no punch. Nothing, except his pride and the crowd chanting, "Ali! Ali!" "I really thought something bad might happen that night," Jerry Izenberg recalls. "And I was praying that it wouldn't be the something that we dread most in boxing. I've been at three fights where fighters died, and it sort of found a home in the back of my mind. I was saying, I don't want this man to get hurt. Whoever won the fight was irrelevant to me."

It wasn't an athletic contest; just a brutal beating that went on and on. Later, some observers claimed that Holmes lay back because of his fondness for Ali. But Holmes was being cautious, not compassionate. "I love the man," he later acknowledged. "But when the bell rung, I didn't even know his name."

"By the ninth round, Ali had stopped fighting altogether," Lloyd Wells remembers. "He was just defending himself, and not doing a good job of that. Then, in the ninth round, Holmes hit him with a punch to the body, and Ali screamed. I never will forget that as long as I live. Ali screamed."

The fight was stopped after eleven rounds. An era in boxing — and an entire historical era — was over. And now, years later, in addition to his more important social significance, Ali is widely recognized as the greatest fighter of all time. He was graced with almost unearthly physical skills, and did everything that his body allowed him to do. In a sport that is often brutal and violent, he cast a long and graceful shadow.

How good was Ali? "In the early days," Ferdie Pacheco recalls, "he fought as though he had a glass

FACING PAGE: *Ali was no match in 1980 for Larry Holmes.*

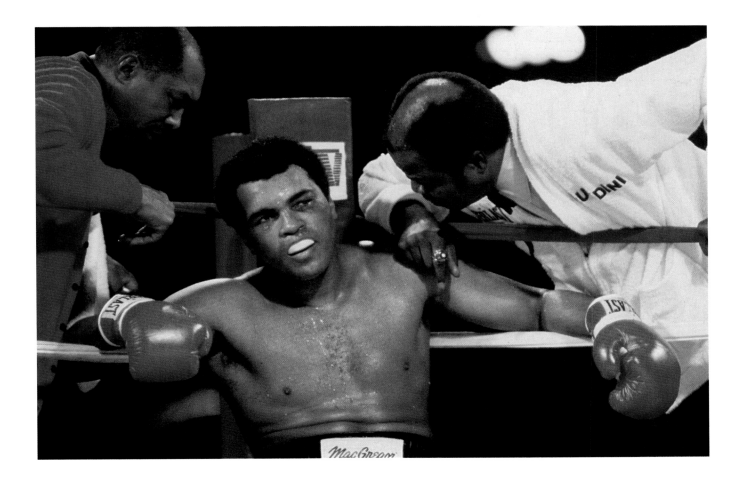

Ali wasn't tarnished by his fight against Larry Holmes. By that point, Ali was above and beyond being tarnished by anything that

happened in a boxing ring. But that fight tarnished boxing terribly, and it troubles me enormously that it was allowed to happen.

Still, I have to say, it infuriates me whenever people use Ali as an example of why boxing should be banned. What would Cassius

Clay have become without boxing?

- - - - - - - - - - -

LOU DIBELLA
(VICE PRESIDENT, TIME WARNER SPORTS)

jaw and was afraid to get hit. He had the hyper reflexes of a frightened man. He was so fast that you had the feeling, 'This guy is scared to death; he can't be that fast normally.' Well, he wasn't scared. He was fast beyond belief and smart. Then he went into exile, and when he came back, he couldn't move like lightning anymore. Everyone wondered, 'What happens now when he gets hit?' That's when we learned something else about him. That sissy-looking, soft-looking, beautiful-looking, child-man was one of the toughest guys who ever lived."

Ali didn't have one-punch knockout power. His most potent offensive weapon was speed — the speed of his jab and straight right hand. But when he sat down on his punches, as he did against Joe Frazier in Manila, he hit harder than most heavyweights. And in addition to his other assets, he had superb foot-work, the ability to take a punch, and all of the intangibles that go into making a great fighter.

"Ali fought all wrong," acknowledges Jerry Izenberg. "Boxing people would say to me, 'Any guy who can do this will beat him. Any guy who can do that will beat him.' And after a while, I started saying back to them, 'So you're telling me that any guy who can outjab the fastest jabber in the world can beat him. Any guy who can slip that jab, which is like lightning, not get hit with a hook off the jab, get inside, and pound on his ribs can beat him. Any guy. Well, you're asking for the greatest fighter who ever lived, so this kid must be pretty good.' "

And on top of everything else, the world never saw Muhammad Ali at his peak as a fighter. When Ali was forced into exile in 1967, he was getting better with virtually every fight. The Ali who fought Cleveland Williams, Ernie Terrell, and Zora Folley was bigger, stronger, more confident, and more skilled than the twenty-two-year-old who, three years earlier, had defeated Sonny Liston. But when Ali returned, his ring skills were diminished. He was markedly slower, and his legs weren't the same.

"I was better when I was young," Ali acknowledged later. "I was more experienced when I was older. I was stronger; I had more belief in myself. Except for Sonny Liston, the men I fought when I was young weren't near the fighters that Joe Frazier and George Foreman were. But I had my speed when I was young. I was faster on my legs, and my hands were faster."

Thus, the world never saw what might have been. What it did see though, in the second half of Ali's career, was an incredibly courageous fighter. Not only did Ali fight his heart out in the ring; he fought the most dangerous foes imaginable. Many champions avoid facing tough challengers. When Joe Louis was champion, he refused to fight certain black contenders. After Joe Frazier defeated Ali, his next defenses were against Terry Daniels and Ron Stander. Once George Foreman won the title, his next bout was against Jose Roman. But Ali had a different creed. "I fought the best, because if you want to be a true champion, you got to show people that you can whup everybody," he proclaimed.

"I don't think there's a fighter in his right mind that wouldn't admire Ali," says Earnie Shavers. "We all dreamed about being just half the fighter that Ali was." And of course, each time Ali entered the ring, the pressure on him was palpable. "It's not like making a movie where, if you mess up, you stop and reshoot," he said shortly before Ali-Frazier III. "When that bell rings and you're out there, the whole world is watching and it's real."

But Ali was more than a great fighter. He was the standard-bearer for boxing's modern era. The sixties promised athletes who were bigger and faster than their predecessors, and Ali was the prototype for that mold. Also, he was part and parcel of the changing economics of boxing. Ali arrived just in time for the advent of satellites and closed circuit television. He carried heavyweight championship boxing beyond the confines of the United States, and popularized the sport around the globe.

●

FACING PAGE: *Howard Cosell (on the right) was a ready foil for Ali at pre-fight weigh-ins.*

Almost always, the public sees boxers as warriors without ever realizing their soft human side. But the whole world saw Ali's humanity. "I was never a boxing fan until Ali came along," is a refrain one frequently hears. And while "the validity of boxing is always hanging by a thread," England's premier boxing writer, Hugh McIlvanney, acknowledges, "Ali was boxing's salvation."

An Ali fight was always an event. Ali put that in perspective when he said, "I truly believe I'm fighting for the betterment of people. I'm not fighting for diamonds or Rolls-Royces or mansions, but to help mankind. Before a fight, I get myself psyched up. It gives me more power, knowing there's so much involved and so many people are gonna be helped by my victory." To which Gil Noble adds, "When Ali got in the ring, there was a lot more at stake than the title. When that man got in the ring, he took all of us with him."

Also, for virtually his entire career, being around Ali was fun. Commenting on young Cassius Clay, Don Elbaum remembers, "I was the matchmaker for a show in Pittsburgh when he fought Charlie Powell. We were staying at a place called Carlton House. And two or three days before the fight, Cassius, which was his name then, decided to visit a black area of Pittsburgh. It was winter, real cold. But he went out, walking the streets, just talking to people. And I've never seen anything like it in my life. When he came back to the hotel around six o'clock, there were three hundred people following him. The Pied Piper couldn't have done any better. And the night of the fight, the weather was awful. There was a blizzard; the schools were shut down. Snow kept falling; it was windy. Conditions were absolutely horrible. And the fight sold out."

Some athletes are engaging when they're young, but lose their charm as their celebrity status grows. But Mike Katz of the *New York Daily News* recalls the day when Ali, at the peak of his popularity, defended his title against Richard Dunn. "On the day of the fight," Katz remembers, "Ali got bored so he decided to hold a press conference. Word got around; Ali came downstairs, and we went to a conference room in the hotel, but it wasn't set up yet. So every member of the press followed him around. We were like mice, going from room to room, until finally the hotel management set us up someplace. And Ali proceeded to have us all in stitches. He imitated every opponent he'd ever fought, including Richard Dunn, who he hadn't fought yet. And he was marvelous. You'd have paid more money to see Muhammad Ali on stage at that point than you'd pay today for Robin Williams."

And Ali retained his charm even as he got old. "The first Ali fight I ever covered," says Ron Borges, "was the one against Leon Spinks, where Ali said it made him look silly to talk up an opponent with only seven professional fights so he wasn't talking. And I said to myself, 'Great. Here I am, a young reporter about to cover the most verbally gifted athlete in history, and the man's not talking.' Anyway, I was at one of Ali's workouts. Ali finished sparring, picked up a microphone, and told us all what he'd said before: 'I'm not talking.' And then he went on for about ninety minutes. Typical Ali; the funniest monologue I've ever heard. And when he was done, he put the microphone down, smiled that incredible smile, and told us all, 'But I'm not talking.'

"I'll always remember the joy of being around Ali," Borges says in closing. "It was fun. And covering the heavyweights isn't much fun anymore. Ali took that with him when he left, and things have been pretty ugly lately."

Muhammad Ali did too much for boxing. And the sport isn't the same without him.

FACING PAGE: *Ali in 1974: A blend of mayhem and magic that carried him deep into the collective psyche of us all.*

When he gave up the championship, he became America's number one role model in the black community. And when he came back, he truly convinced us all that, if you stand up and speak out for what is right, you will win in the end; that as tough as it is, even though you're black and poor,

HEARD THE TERM "EXILE" USED IN CONNECTION WITH ALI'S INABILITY TO DEFEND HIS TITLE FOR A CONSIDERABLE AMOUNT OF TIME, BUT I NEVER THOUGHT OF IT AS AN EXILE. IT WAS MORE JUST A RIP-OFF AND A ROBBERY. ALI DIDN'T GO ANYPLACE; HE WAS STILL HERE. THE TITLE DIDN'T GO ANYPLACE. THE SYMBOL OF WHO IS TRULY THE CHAMPION OF BOXING IS A BELT THAT'S GOT DIAMONDS AND STUFF, AND ALL THROUGH THE WHOLE PERIOD YOU'RE TALKING ABOUT, ALI HAD THAT BELT IN HIS LIVING ROOM. NO, BOXING WAS IN EXILE. BOXING WENT AWAY FROM ITS OWN STANDARDS. BOXING WENT AWAY FROM ITS OWN CREED. BOXING WENT AWAY FROM THE CHAMPIONSHIP BELT. IT'S NONSENSE TO TALK ABOUT ALI BEING IN EXILE. ALI WAS RIGHT HERE

OSCAR BROWN, JR.

SETTING THE STAGE FOR ALI-FRAZIER I:

There has never been, nor will there ever be, a build-up to a fight like that one. The term "Fight of the Century" has been cheapened through overuse, but that one really was. In fact, it might have been the "Fight of All Time."

ANTHONY CARTER PAIGE
(PRESIDENT, BOXING WRITERS ASSOC. OF AMERICA)

That was the most exciting night of boxing ever. It was electric. Just to be there meant everything. People who were absolute superstars were sitting in the twentieth row. Thousands of people lined up outside Madison Square Garden, just to watch everyone come in.

BOB ARUM
(WHO PROMOTED MANY OF ALI'S FIGHTS)

I've covered sports for forty-five years. I've covered every sport you can name. And no moment I've ever seen had the electricity of those two men coming down the aisle and entering the ring that night.

JERRY IZENBERG
(COLUMNIST, *NEWARK STAR-LEDGER*)

ABOVE: Ali met frequently with the press as Ali-Frazier I approached.
RIGHT: Then Ali and "Smokin' Joe" did battle for the first time under referee Arthur Mercante's watchful eye.

The biggest-money fight to date was Evander Holyfield versus George Foreman, which worldwide grossed

about eighty million dollars. If you could put Ali-Frazier I in a time capsule and promote it today with

today's technology, that fight would gross close to two hundred million dollars. Think about that for a

moment; it's a staggering number. Two hundred million dollars for an hour of television. And with honest

"THERE'S NO NUMBER WE WOULDN'T REACH"

managers and an honest promoter, roughly ninety million dollars of that would go to the fighters. If

Muhammad Ali were fighting and well-managed today, he'd be the richest athlete, and maybe the richest

entertainer, ever. Whatever it took to get him, Time Warner would pay. We wouldn't be outbid by anybody.

There's no number we wouldn't reach. Whatever it took, we would get Muhammad Ali.

SETH ABRAHAM
(PRESIDENT, TIME WARNER SPORTS)

FACING PAGE: *March 8, 1971: At Madison Square Garden in Ali-Frazier I, Joe Frazier's left hook landed time and time again.*

ABOVE AND FACING PAGE: *Ali's Deer Lake, Pennsylvania training camp, built in 1972, was almost always open to the public and became his home away from home.*

My father, who's eighty-eight years old now, isn't the most liberal person in the world. He was a construction worker for most of his life, and he never liked people who talked a lot. But when Ali was willing to go to jail for his beliefs that got my father's attention. He told me, "You know, I don't agree with what this guy is doing, but he's all right. You get very few chances to be a man in life, and this guy takes advantage of them." And I'll tell you something else. My father voted for George Wallace in 1968, and for George McGovern in 1972. That's quite a change, and I have to believe that watching Muhammad Ali was part of what influenced him.

— — — — — — — — — — —

RON BORGES
(BOXING WRITER FOR THE BOSTON GLOBE)

Ali and his second wife, Belinda, posed with their four children at Ali's training camp in Deer Lake (top left). The camp luxury of quiet moments (top right), *but he seldom took advantage of them, preferring to stay active at all times (bo* PAGE: "I have a soft spot in my heart for old people," was Ali's explanation for his frequent visits to old-age homes.

I've never gone through the formality of playing Russian roulette. But about as close as I ever came to it was getting on a bus with Ali. You don't want to be on a bus with Ali for more than an hour. Because after an hour, Ali wants to drive and then you're in trouble. He loves to drive, and he loves to drive fast. One time, we were in London. We were standing in line with everybody else to get on a bus. By everybody else, I mean the unsuspecting people of London, who were waiting to go home at the end of the day. Ali put his money in like everybody else, and asked the bus driver, "Can I drive?" And the bus driver, of course, said, "Muhammad Ali; why certainly, you can drive." And the people on the bus were yelling, "Great! Great! Great! Muhammad Ali is going to drive us." And Angelo Dundee was saying, "No! No! No! Don't let him drive. You don't understand." But the will of the people could not be ignored, so Ali got behind the wheel. There was a terrific grinding of gears. The bus took off at a terrific rate of speed. And Ali had it pretty much under control, except for the fact that this was London, so while he was driving on the right-hand side of the road, the traffic was coming straight at him.

JERRY IZENBERG

FACING PAGE AND ABOVE: *Ali takes a turn at the wheel of the press bus for reporters visiting his training camp at Deer Lake. It was a marked improvement over an earlier ride when a chagrined Cassius Clay demonstrated his road skills by driving his bus into a ditch.* PREVIOUS PAGES: *Early morning, alone on the road, at Deer Lake in 1978.*

Norman Mailer decided one night in Zaire that he was going to do roadwork with Ali. Ali told him, "If you want to run with me, you can. But I run five miles in the jungle, and if you get tired, there are no cabs to take you back." Well, Norman's afflicted by the need to always be part of the scene and assert his macho image. So about four o'clock in the morning, he went out to run with Ali. He ran for maybe a quarter of a mile, and then he fell behind, totally out of gas. In a jet black jungle. There wasn't even a firefly, just total darkness. And then Norman heard this colossal roar. And if there's one distinctive sound in this world, it's the sound of a lion roaring in the jungle. You cannot mistake it for anything else. It's big and it's hungry and it rattles your bones. So Norman thought that his end had come. He didn't know whether to try to outrun it — he certainly couldn't outrun a lion — or ease on down the road, or just stand still and hope the lion went by. So he stood still for a while; and then he decided that, since he hadn't been eaten yet, he might as well try to get back to the compound, which he did. Ali had come back by this time. The sun was rising. And Norman told him that the literary world had come close to losing one of its great geniuses, because he'd almost been eaten by a lion. He's telling Ali, "There's a lion out there; you shouldn't be running." And Ali says, "Yeah, I know. There's a whole family of lions out there. They won't bother you." So Norman asks if Ali is crazy. And Ali takes him by the arm, and walks him down the road about a quarter of a mile to where the lions were caged in President Mobutu's zoo.

FERDIE PACHECO

(ALI'S RING PHYSICIAN FOR MOST OF HIS BOXING CAREER)

ABOVE AND FACING PAGE: *Preparing to fight George Foreman, Ali was readily accessible to the people of Zaire.*
PREVIOUS PAGES: *In Zaire, word of Ali's arrival at any site brought thousands of followers to the scene.*

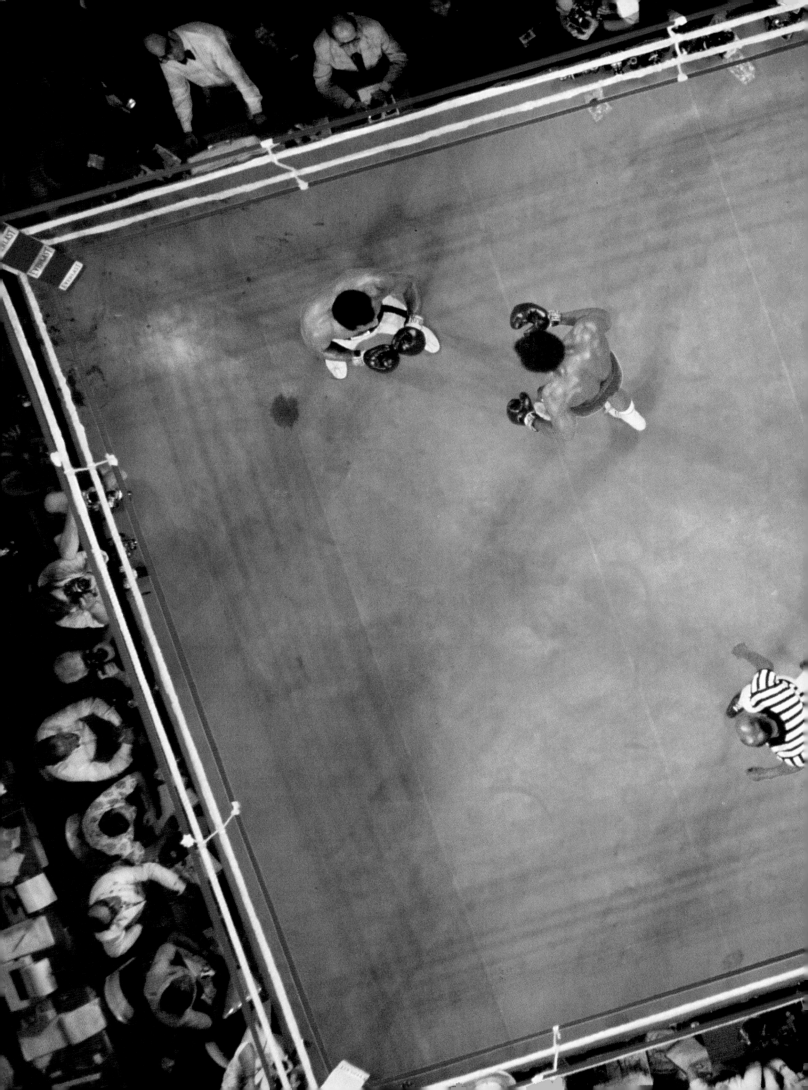

You know, it used to be the Belgian Congo. And then they had a revolution, kicked the Belgians out, and renamed everything. The name of the country was changed to Zaire. The Congo River became the Zaire River. Congo became a dirty name. But it was still a police state, and Mobutu had censors who read everything that went out on the wire. Anyway, the night before the fight, they had a big jazz concert in the same stadium where the fight was going to be. One of the writers reviewed it, and wrote about how great this guy was on the conga drums. And a censor changed it to the Zaire drums. I'll never forget that; the Zaire drums.

HAROLD CONRAD

LEFT: *Muhammad Ali versus George Foreman,*
October 30, 1974.
ABOVE: *A last-minute prayer.*

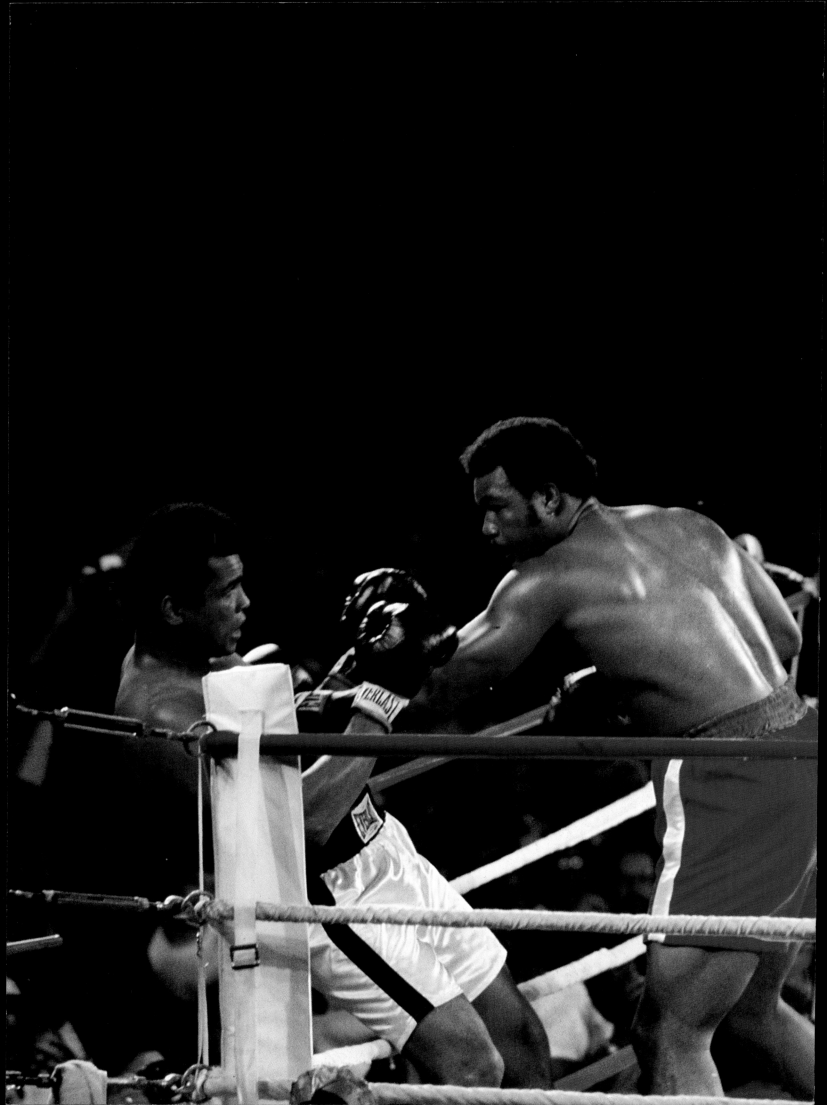

After the fight, I went to Ali's dressing room to congratulate him, and then I went to Foreman's. Archie Moore was the only other person there. There was Foreman, Archie, me, and Foreman's dog. George kept looking in the mirror at the lumps on his face, as though he couldn't believe what he saw. Then we went back to the hotel, and George got a telephone call from Jim Marshall, who had been in three or four Super Bowls with the Vikings and never won. Marshall did his best to console him. And Foreman said, "Don't worry; I'll be alright." But you could see, he was totally bewildered by it all.

JIM BROWN

FACING PAGE: *Foreman's strategy was to pin Ali against the ropes. But when cornered, Ali employed a "rope-a-dope" strategy to lean back out of harm's way.*
ABOVE: *Seconds from victory as referee Zack Clayton nears the count of ten.*

If you wanted to make an allegory about good and evil and patience and virtue, after that fight in Zaire you

really could. It was like God waited until it was over. And then there was a tremendous clap of thunder, and

we were caught in the worst kind of African cloudburst. It was the most intense rainstorm I've ever seen.

If it had happened two hours earlier, the fight would have been wiped out. There were terrible winds; flash-

flooding. And then, as suddenly as it had come, the storm was over. Dawn arrived; the sun came up. And

A STORM IN ZAIRE

it was like the whole history of "I ain't got no quarrel with them Vietcong" and the hatred and the ugliness

had been washed away. And I remember that morning, standing with Ali by the Zaire River. There were just

a couple of us. The air was sticky sweet with that aroma of African flowers, and the ground was damp from

that tremendous storm. Ali was looking out over the river, and he said to us, "You'll never know how long

I waited for this. You'll never know what this means to me."

- - - - - - - - - - -

JERRY IZENBERG

FACING PAGE: *Ali, captured during a reflective moment, looking out over the Zaire river.*

Ali could walk up to a piano and entertain you, like you'd swear he could play the piano. He memorized how to play a few

songs, and he'd sit there and play just enough to impress you. Little Richard was his favorite — "Bop-bop-a-lu-bop-a-wop-bam-

boom!" He'd play, and he'd sing; and by the time he got through, you'd say, "Wow; this guy is really talented." But once he did

that, he couldn't play nothing else; not at gunpoint if his life depended on it.

- - - - - - - - - - -

PAT PATTERSON

ABOVE: *When Ali sat down at the piano, it was mostly for show.*

121

When I was growing up in Louisville, I used to daydream all the time about being successful in boxing and being famous. But one time I remember in particular. Floyd Patterson was heavyweight champion of the world. I was at the Olympics in Rome. And I went to sleep in my room, pretending I was heavyweight champion. This was even before I won the gold medal. But I lay in bed, pretending I was famous, pretending everyone liked me and looked up to me the way I looked up to Floyd Patterson. And God blessed me. My dream came true. But I got different dreams now. Now I dream about doing something to stop all the hating in the world. I dream about feeding people who are hungry. I dream about children learning how to read and write. And sometimes, when I'm really dreaming, I dream about being a rock star like Elvis or Little Richard.

——————

MUHAMMAD ALI

ABOVE: *Ali posed in a robe bearing the legend "People's Champion," given to him by Elvis Presley in 1973.*

Ali and Joe were like peanut butter and jelly. They needed each other to make things happen.

BUTCH LEWIS

ABOVE: *October 1, 1975: With Joe Frazier pressing the action in Manila, moments where Ali could maneuver freely on his way to victory were few and far between. At the end of round fourteen, Frazier's chief cornerman stopped the fight.*
FACING PAGE: *The price of victory was all too evident on Ali's face at the post-fight press conference.*

MADISON SQUARE GARDEN IN ASSOCIATION WITH TOP RANK INC. PRESENTS
SEPT. 28, 1976
WORLD HEAVYWEIGHT

Debunking Some Myths About Ali:

- Ali did not originate the phrase, "No Vietcong ever called me nigger." That was misattributed to him after he said, "I ain't got no quarrel with them Vietcong."

- Ali never threw his Olympic gold medal into the Ohio River. That was one of many allegorical tales included in the film *The Greatest* by ghostwriter Richard Durham. Either the medal was stolen or Ali lost it.

- Ali was genuinely fond of Howard Cosell. He appreciated the fact that Cosell spoke out on his behalf in the sixties, and he admired Cosell both as a professional reporter and a truly original character

FACING PAGE AND ABOVE: *Ali had definite plans for Ken Norton, but wound up prevailing in their third bout by the narrowest of decisions.*

ABOVE: *In between fights in the seventies, Ali turned actor in* The Greatest *(top) and* Freedom Road *(bottom).*
FACING PAGE: *Ali mugs for the camera.*

I see Muhammad Ali very much as a spiritual leader. You know, here's a man who can go into the Islamic world, which is huge beyond our imagination, and you need troops to clear the way for him. I don't know if there's anybody on earth who could go to those countries and draw the crowds that Muhammad Ali can draw. To tell you the truth — and I don't mean to be irreverent — I doubt the Pope could draw crowds as large as Muhammad Ali. I think he's probably the single most powerful religious figure in this country, and maybe in the world.

ALEX HALEY

LEFT: *Ali was greeted as a conquering hero in Bangladesh in 1978.*

I was in Ali's dressing room after he lost to Leon Spinks. He'd been beaten; no question about it. But it was the usual situation, where all his people were gathered around him, saying, "Bad decision. You won that fight, champ." And so on and so forth; the usual nonsense. Ali was lying on a rubdown table, not saying a thing. And all of a sudden, he rose up. He sat up straight, and shouted, "Shut up! I lost!" You could hear a pin drop. And then he lay down again. But that was Ali. As much as he always wanted to win, he could accept losing with dignity and grace.

RON BORGES

FACING PAGE: *February 15, 1978: Ali on the ropes in a losing effort against Leon Spinks.*
ABOVE: *Seven months after being dethroned, Ali returned to defeat Spinks and capture the heavyweight championship for an unprecedented third time.*

Don't think that I went to bed those nights and had a good sleep, because I didn't. I was fighting Muhammad Ali. I knew I could beat this guy, but I never knew what trick he had up his sleeve. And it was mind-boggling. Everywhere I went, there was Muhammad Ali. I mean, I got on the airplane, and who do I see on the airplane? Ali. I get to Las Vegas; and all these newspaper people, camera people, critics; who do they run to? Ali. We went through the casino, and all I heard was, "Ali! Ali!" And Ali could put a lot of things on your mind if you listened to him. He'd shadow box, and show you how quick he was. He'd pull his shirt up, and show you how thin he'd gotten. He was always saying, "Hey, I told you with Sonny Liston; I told you with George Foreman." And if you listened, you'd believe him. You'd say, "What the hell am I fighting this guy for?" So it was rough for me to sleep at night. I was fighting Muhammad Ali.

LARRY HOLMES

LEFT: *In 1980, before the Holmes fight, the self described "Dark Gable" grew a mustache to cover up an inch-long gash on his upper lip suffered while sparring.*
FOLLOWING PAGES: *October 2, 1980. An aging Muhammad Ali was virtually defenseless as Larry Holmes pounded him against the ropes and captured the title in the eleventh round.*

The greatness or the smallness of a man does not depend upon his education or his wealth or other outer things. Regardless of how wealthy a man is, regardless of how educated he is; if his heart is not great, then he cannot be great. It is the heart that makes one great or small.

MUHAMMAD ALI

ABOVE: *Ali was on the verge of retiring from boxing, when he and his mother met with reporters just prior to his fight against Trevor Berbick.*

If I say a cow can lay an egg, don't argue with me. Go get the skillet.

- - - - - - - - - - -

MUHAMMAD ALI

ABOVE: *Visiting a magic shop in New York, Ali "levitated" for a watchful crowd.*

Ali left the studio announcing to everybody that he had murdered this famous debater; that there was nothing left of me; that there wasn't anybody in history who had been knocked out more definitively than I had. And he said it often. For two or three months, every time he had a press conference, he would mention it.

WILLIAM BUCKLEY, JR.
(ON THE AFTERMATH OF HIS DEBATE WITH MUHAMMAD ALI ON "FIRING LINE")

CLOCKWISE FROM TOP LEFT: *The spoils of victory on a worldwide stage. Ali with Gerald Ford, Henry Kissinger, Jimmy*

Oxford University, that's a big university, wants me to be a professor of poetry and some kind of social something. They say I won't have to go there but once or twice a year for a lecture. And the salary they pay won't pay my telephone bills, but I said I'd come over for the prestige. Very few boxers can be professors at Oxford University.

MUHAMMAD ALI

ABOVE: *Ali and Jacqueline Onassis shared a unique bond. They became famous in 1960 as Cassius Clay and Jackie Kennedy, yet ultimately were known throughout the world by different names.*

TOP: *Ali with his third wife, Veronica, and their daughters, Hana and Laila.*
BOTTOM: *Three years later, a dutiful father took daughters Hana and Laila for a ride outside their Los Angeles home.*
FACING PAGE: *Ali in 1984, with the first eight of his nine children.*

Everyone has good and bad inside of them. And with Ali, almost always, the better man inside won.

MARION BOYKIN
(BOXING WRITER)

There's no cruelty left in him. As a fighter, it was necessary. As a fighter, you're supposed to be cruel. In the ring, if you're a nice guy, you get knocked out in a hurry. But that cruelty is no longer a part of him.

DAVE KINDRED
(COLUMNIST FOR THE *ATLANTA JOURNAL-CONSTITUTION*)

PART THREE

MUHAMMAD ALI'S LIFE TODAY

Not long ago, Muhammad Ali was at a party, surrounded by the usual chaos that accompanies his

presence. Men who would rarely think of hugging another man fell into his embrace. Women were asking

for kisses. There were requests for autographs and photographs, when amidst it all, a mother brought her

four-year-old daughter over to Ali. "Do you know who this is?" she asked her child.

The four-year-old nodded reverentially. "It's the Easter Bunny," she said.

That moment speaks volumes. Muhammad Ali, who was once viewed as "a dangerous, militant,

black-nationalist revolutionary," is now all good things to all people.

FACING PAGE: *Once a feared warrior, Ali is now a venerated figure who evokes feelings of love and respect throughout the world.*
ABOVE: *Ali attends services regularly, as he did on this 1987 visit to a Chicago mosque.*

With its mixture of comedy, tragedy, and melodrama, Ali's life has been one of Shakespearean proportions. He careened through his first forty years like a man on Rollerblades. Or as William Buckley, Jr. later said, "Ali was always on a flying trapeze, and he did it without nets."

Ali's pace is slower now, but he still leads a full life. He and his wife, Lonnie, celebrate their tenth wedding anniversary on November 19, 1996. Those closest to Muhammad believe that Lonnie, more than anyone else, deserves credit for the happiness and serenity that Ali experiences today. Another enormously important person in Ali's life is his closest friend, Howard Bingham. "Life wouldn't be right without Howard Bingham around me," Ali acknowledged recently.

"Howard would do or die for Muhammad," explains Lonnie Ali. "They're like brothers. They can't be separated or not hear from each other for any length of time without missing each other. No matter where we are, we talk to Howard just about every day. He and Muhammad have been put in a lot of different situations, and Howard adapts to everything." Then Lonnie adds, "Howard has also always gotten along well with Muhammad's wives; each and every one of us. But he has a little saying he likes to say; and it's funny because it's been true — "I was here before you came, and I'll be here when you're gone." To which Bingham responds quickly, "But Lonnie is here to stay. She's the best thing that ever happened to Ali, and Ali knows it."

The biggest change in Muhammad's life in recent years has been the addition of another child to his family. Ali had eight children (seven daughters and a son) prior to his marriage to Lonnie. Then in 1991, he and Lonnie decided to adopt an infant boy. "One of the things that has been constant through Muhammad Ali's life is that he loves children," says Dr. Betty Shabazz (the widow of Malcolm X). "His children, other people's children. I don't think that Muhammad Ali could have too many children." Asaad Amin Ali is now five years old, and the apple of his father's eye. "Muhammad adores Saadi, and Saadi adores Muhammad," says Lonnie Ali. "And the one thing that still always lights up Muhammad's eyes is children, which is one of the many reasons that I thank Allah for Asaad."

Ali's health is a matter of public record, and is monitored regularly for any change. He suffers from Parkinson's Syndrome, which refers to a series of symptoms, the most apparent of which are slurred speech, trembling of the hands, and a facial "mask." The condition was brought on by blows to the head that destroyed brain cells necessary to produce a substance called dopamine. Former heavyweight champion Tim Witherspoon speaks for his brethren when he says, "When I see Ali today, I wish the way he is now, it wouldn't be." But Ali's condition is not life-threatening; there are no intellectual deficits; and Muhammad's thought processes are clear. The things that were once evident in his voice still burn brightly within him. And even though he no longer shouts, his warmth, humor, folly, and wisdom are still audible to anyone who listens.

Because of Ali's physical condition, there's a tendency on the part of some to feel awkward in his presence and act protectively of him in public. But Lou DiBella of Time Warner Sports puts the matter in perspective when he says, "I hear people talking about how they feel sorry for Ali, and isn't what happened

FACING PAGE: *Muhammad at home in Berrien Springs with Lonnie Ali and their son, Asaad Amin Ali.*

to him terrible. But to be honest with you, I don't have that reaction. Sure it makes me sad that his health isn't what it used to be. But he's still the same person. He still enjoys life. The sense of decency and principles that drove him in the sixties still drive him. What does bother me though, is the way some people react to Ali — like he's infirm or mentally deficient or in need of care. Watching people react to Ali like that depresses me. Seeing Ali himself is still very much uplifting to me."

Of all the things associated with Parkinson's Syndrome, Ali himself is most concerned by his slurred speech. But he accepts his condition as God's will, and says firmly, "God never gives anyone a burden that's too heavy to carry."

Lonnie Ali concurs and says, "If Muhammad has slipped a bit recently, it might not be completely physical in nature. When Muhammad's mother died [in August 1994], it was a turning point for Muhammad. The day after the funeral, he got very quiet. At first, I thought it was a natural part of mourning, and that his spirits would improve with time. But I have to say that his mother's death is still very much on Muhammad's mind. Also," Lonnie continues, "there are times when Muhammad allows his physical condition to take things away from him unnecessarily. He doesn't speak as often as he should; partly because he doesn't like the way he sounds, and partly because he can accomplish most of what he wants to accomplish by communicating nonverbally. Still, I'd have to say that Muhammad isn't as self-confident as he used to be, and still should be. Sometimes I think back to how in love he was with the camera, and how in love the camera was with him. And it makes me sad to see the way Muhammad sometimes shies away from cameras today."

But to compensate for what he might have lost, Ali has gained in other ways. He's more at peace with himself now than in the past, and a great deal of that has to do with the evolution of his religious beliefs. When Muhammad was young, he had the tendency to bend the teachings of his religion to accommodate what he wanted to do. Now the converse is true. Each night, before going to bed, Ali asks himself, "If God were to judge me based just on what I did today, would I go to heaven or hell?" And he lives his life accordingly.

Thus, Lonnie Ali can say, "Over the past ten years, Muhammad has flowered spiritually beyond anything I saw in him before we were married. There's an underlying spiritual quality about him that wasn't there when he was younger. Muhammad believes that he's on the path to heaven. And while it's not my judgment to make, I believe he'll get there."

A typical Ali day varies greatly, depending on whether he's at home or traveling. Muhammad spends much of his time on an eighty-eight-acre farm near Berrien Springs, a small town in southwest Michigan near the Indiana border. When at home, Ali rises at 5 A.M. for the first of five daily prayers. Then he goes downstairs and spends several hours autographing pamphlets that he'll give to people he meets during the course of his day. The pamphlets explain different facets of Islam. "I'm not trying to convert anybody," Ali says. "Only God can do that. I just want to open people's minds, so they'll think about God and Islam."

FACING PAGE: *Muhammad and Lonnie on the road* (top) *and at home in the kitchen* (bottom).

Ali doesn't say as much now as he did before, but he doesn't have to. He said it all, and said it when almost no one

After breakfast, Ali might go for a walk. Much of his day will be spent doing errands, reading the Qur'an, watching television, and answering mail. The house is large and comfortable, but not ostentatious. People and spiritual matters have always meant more to Ali than wealth and material things.

But away from home, Ali's life is less tranquil. Whenever Ali walks down a street, everyone he passes knows exactly who he is. Think about that for a moment. It's awesome. And virtually every one of those people wants to reach out and touch Ali in some way, if only for a moment, and will remember that moment until the day they die. "You can talk about George Washington," says publicist Irving Rudd. "You can talk about the Kennedys. But the closest thing to a king that this country has ever had is Muhammad Ali. And it goes beyond that, because the whole world is in love with Ali."

Thus, it's fortunate that, after his belief in God, the thing that most sustains Muhammad is the outpouring of love he receives from the people he meets every day. He is cognizant of their affection and regards it, not as a burden, but as an honor and a responsibility to treat people right. "All their life, people will remember when they met me," Ali says. "And I want their memories to be nice." To which Lloyd Wells adds, "Ali loves to travel. He can't wait to get to the airport. Most times, he's not really concerned about where he's going or what it's for. It's always the same thing; signing autographs, taking pictures. People from all walks of life want him. There's banquets for charities, school groups, and religious organizations. He always says, 'I just want to go home and rest.' But after a while at home, he's ready to go again."

Ali's sojourns have taken him around the world on numerous occasions. And during the course of his travels, he has met more heads of state than most heads of state meet in a lifetime. His missions have been designed to accomplish goals as diverse as freeing hostages held in Iraq, to drawing attention to the plight of famine victims in Sudan. He has had audiences with five presidents of the United States — Gerald Ford, Jimmy Carter, Ronald Reagan, George Bush, and Bill Clinton. A frequent visitor to the Middle East, he has conferred with Anwar Sadat in Egypt, King Fahd in Saudi Arabia, Hafez Assad in Syria, King Hussein in Jordan, Muammar Qaddafi in Libya, and Saddam Hussein in Iraq. Ali has been received by Premier Deng Xiaping in China, President Abdur Rahman Biswas in Bangladesh, and Prime Minister Indira Gandhi in India. His travels in Africa have included visits with Nelson Mandela of South Africa, Robert Mugabe of Zimbabwe, Mobutu Sese Seko of Zaire, Daniel arap Moi of Kenya, and Kwame Nkrumah of Ghana. Soviet leaders Leonid Brezhnev and Mikhail Gorbachev have hosted Ali, as have Cuba's Fidel Castro, Haiti's François Duvalier and Jean-Claude Duvalier, Ferdinand Marcos of the Philippines, and Morocco's King Hassan II. In addition, Ali has enjoyed audiences with Pope John Paul II in the Vatican and Queen Elizabeth II at Buckingham Palace.

The first six months of 1996 were typical of Ali's pace. Between January 1 and June 30, he set foot on five continents and spent 113 out of 182 days on the road. One particularly demanding stretch began with an April 2 trip to Louisville, where Ali met with civic leaders who are planning a Muhammad Ali Museum and Education Center. The next day, he flew to Saudi Arabia; stayed there for a week; returned to Michigan on April 11; left home again for Japan on April 13; and flew back to the United States from Japan on the

FACING PAGE: *Ali prepares for one of five daily prayers, with his daughter Maryum, beside him.*

morning of April 18 so he could be the guest of honor at a fundraising dinner in New Jersey that night.

Ali on the road overwhelms the imagination. A middle-aged woman stops him on the street, and breaks down in tears as she recounts how Muhammad once autographed a photo for her son, who was in the hospital dying of cancer. Four teenagers who are driving by come to a screeching halt, jump out of their car, and plead for autographs. A young woman covers her mouth with her hand and gasps, "Oh my God! You're real!" Often, superstar celebrities intimidate, and people are afraid to approach them. "But Ali opens his arms right up," marvels Larry Holmes. "People don't have to approach him. He approaches them, and makes them feel comfortable."

"As the years have gone by," says TV commentator Dick Schaap, "I think it's become harder and harder to be Muhammad Ali. It's probably the toughest role that anybody has had to play in the twentieth century. And to play that role twenty-four hours a day, day after day, year after year; I think that's taken as much of a toll on him as the punches." Still, Ali continues to give of himself in truly unique ways.

"One night, several years ago," remembers Lou DiBella, "I took my wife to dinner in Manhattan. And as we were walking to the restaurant, I saw something close to a mob on the sidewalk. It was a crowd of people around Muhammad Ali, who was signing autographs. Anyway, my wife and I had dinner, and when we came out of the restaurant, Ali was still there, playing with kids, posing for pictures, signing for everyone who came up to him. I think about that now, when I look at today's athletes, who in the larger scheme of things mean absolutely nothing, who make millions of dollars, who won't take five seconds to give a kid an autograph. And I compare today's so-called 'superstars' with Ali: a man in his fifties with Parkinson's Syndrome, standing on the street that night, embracing every person he met."

152

"It's gratifying for Muhammad to see the way people respond to him," says Lonnie Ali. "And what's even more gratifying is the way young people who weren't even born when Muhammad was fighting are drawn to him. These are five- and six-year-old children, who come up to Muhammad and hug him. And it's truly a blessing from God that the love Muhammad has for people and the love people have for him keeps growing from generation to generation, and that every new generation of children seems to know who Muhammad is."

Yet through it all, Ali has retained a quality that most people once thought he didn't have — his humility. "Ali has an awareness that he's somebody gigantic in this world," says Ferdie Pacheco. "But the truth is, he's remarkably humble; and it's not an artificial humility. As far as using ego in the sense of a Hollywood actor or some superstar athlete who's puffed up by his fame and self-importance, there's none of that. 'I'm the great Ali; give me a hotel room.' Never. 'I'm Ali; get me on this airplane, even if you have to throw someone else off.' Not a chance. He's just not like that."

And Ron Borges recalls a moment that puts Ali in further perspective. "I was in Miami for the Super Bowl a couple of years ago," Borges reminisces. "It was a Friday night, and I was on a bus full of sportswriters who were about to leave for one of those big Super Bowl parties. Anyway, I looked up, and there was Ali getting on the bus. And the first thing Ali did when he got on was reach out and shake hands with

FACING PAGE: *In 1992, Ali celebrated his fiftieth birthday in Los Angeles at a star-studded television gala, surrounded by his wife, his mother, and his nine children.*

If You Want To Be A Hero:

- **You must achieve something substantial.**

- **It helps if you've overcome enormous odds or struck down a hated foe.**

- **There must be an element of risk that has been met head-on.**

- **Heroes most often "do it alone."**

- **Observers must identify with the hero's cause.**

- **A hero places principles and loyalty above personal gain.**

- **Personal magnetism, good looks, and charisma are desirable.**

the bus driver. And of course, not a single one of us on the bus except for Ali had in any way acknowledged the driver. Then we got to the party; we walked in; and the first thing Ali did was shake hands with two waiters who were at the door. Don Shula [then the Miami Dolphins head coach] saw Ali and came running over, but Ali stood there talking with the waiters, and Shula had to wait his turn. And that's the way Ali was the entire night. All the little people — the waiters, the busboys, the people that most of us never bother to think about — Ali stopped for every one of them."

And so it is that Muhammad Ali — who impacted upon the world first as a fighter, and then as a social, political, and religious figure — now influences others most as a person. "I remember a conversation I had with Ali way back in the sixties," recalls Mort Sharnik, formerly of *Sports Illustrated*. "He told me, 'I love everybody; we're all God's children. But black people have special needs. They're my people and they really do need love, so my love is focused on them.' " Now though, Ali's love is spread equally among all people. And those who have interacted with him throughout his life recognize that fact and respond in kind:

- Earnie Shavers: *Ali's got a heart as big as all outdoors and a love that encompasses all people. He's as pretty on the inside as he is on the outside. Always has been; always will be.*
- Harold Conrad: *Ali is a decent man, a kind man; and it doesn't do you any harm to be around one of those. You've got to pick up some of it. Sometimes I wish I could be more like him.*
- Ralph Boston: *If a young boy were to ask me today, "Why should I care about Muhammad Ali?" I'd tell him, "Because Ali cares about you." That might be hard for some people to understand, but that's the way Ali is. He cares about every single person on this planet.*
- Larry Holmes: *If you treated Ali right, he'd treat you right. And if you didn't treat him right, he'd still treat you right. That's just one reason why people love Ali.*
- Jim Brown: *Ali loved goodness. And when he saw goodness, he didn't let color or religion stand in the way.*
- Howard Bingham: *Ali loves people, and people love him. And that's what life is all about.*
- Hugh McIlvanney: *Ali is more than a great man. He's a good man. And good people are hard to find.*
- John Carlos: *Muhammad Ali is love.*

155

Because of his spirit, Muhammad Ali today is not just a memory but a powerful vibrant force. Once the greatest fighter in the world, he is now, first and foremost, a man of peace. He believes that God put him on earth to be kind to people and bring love into their lives. And he is firmly devoted to that cause.

"This man is here for a reason," Lonnie Ali says of her husband. "He has a mission to perform, and I believe that a big part of that mission is to teach people about love. In the past, Muhammad gave of his time, his worldly possessions, even his blood. Now he's giving people the gift of love. Muhammad can walk anywhere on earth, meet anyone, and find a bond that will unite them. And I believe in my heart that this is why Muhammad is still here."

In the sixties, Muhammad Ali was the symbol of a divided America. Now, it would be the fulfillment of his fondest wish to serve as the symbol of a united world. Meanwhile, Ali enjoys a status that has been conferred upon only a handful of men and women who have walked this planet. He has become immortal in his own lifetime.

FACING PAGE: *Muhammad and Lonnie share a reflective moment by the pond on their Michigan farm.*

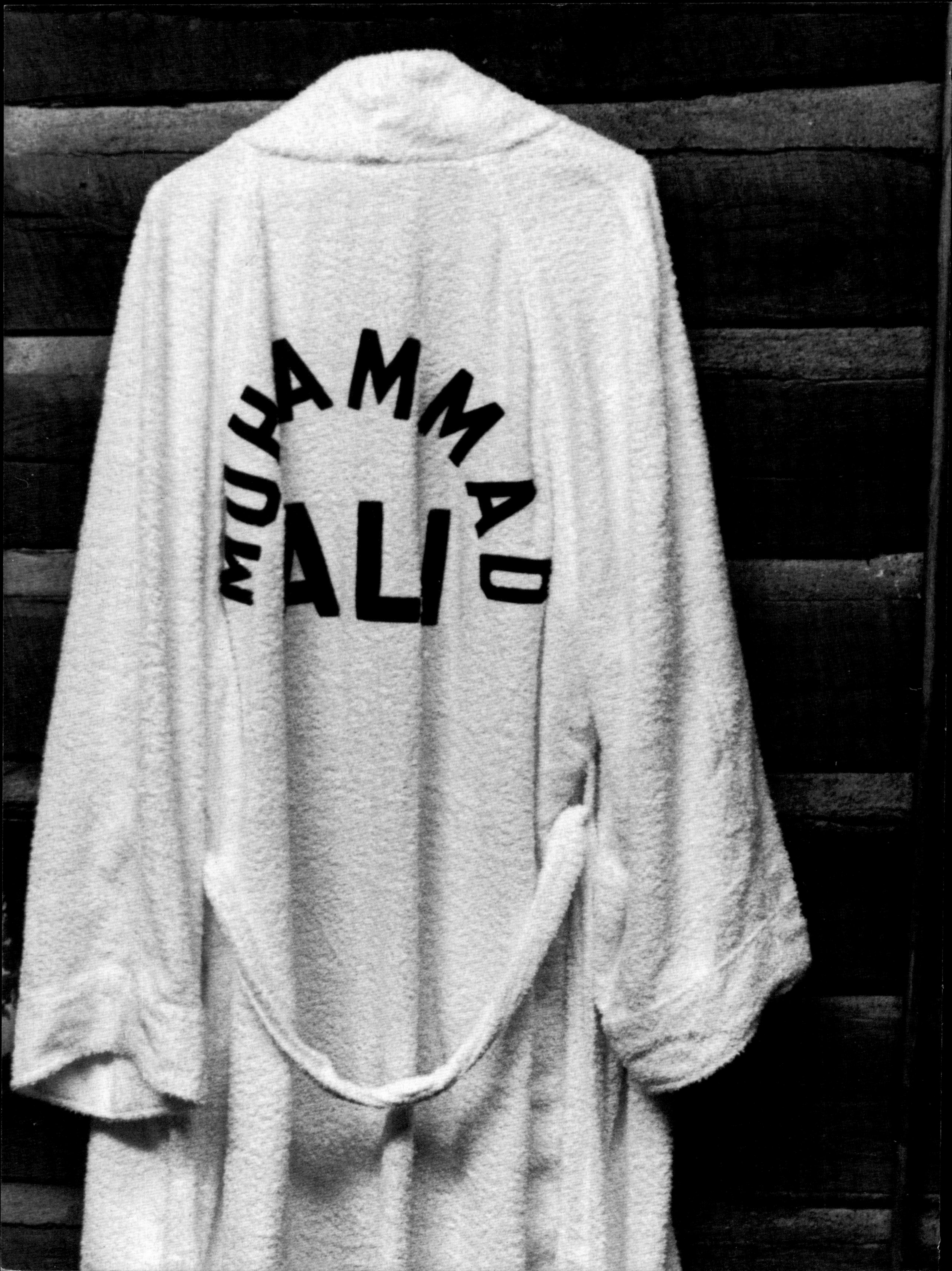
MUHAMMAD
ALI

ALI INJECTED GOD INTO THE ARENA. WHENEVER YOU SAW ALI AT THE END OF A FIGHT, BEFORE HE SAID ANYTHING ELSE, HE WOULD GIVE ALL PRAISE TO ALLAH. HE INJECTED RELIGION. HE INJECTED FAITH. HE INJECTED BELIEF. AND THAT TURNED MY GRANDMOTHER ON AND MY GREAT-GRANDMOTHER ON. EVEN THOUGH HE WAS A MUSLIM, HE TURNED ON THE BAPTIST CHURCH AND CHURCH PEOPLE LIKE NOBODY HAD EVER TURNED THEM ON BEFORE. AND I'LL TELL YOU SOMETHING ELSE. IF PEOPLE FROM OUTER SPACE CAME TO EARTH AND WE HAD TO GIVE THEM ONE REPRESENTATIVE OF OUR SPECIES TO SHOW THEM OUR PHYSICAL PROWESS, OUR SPIRITUALITY, OUR DECENCY, OUR WARMTH, OUR KINDNESS, OUR HUMOR, AND MOST OF ALL OUR CAPACITY TO LOVE — IT WOULD BE ALI.

DICK GREGORY

To me, Muhammad Ali is a totally spiritual person.
It doesn't have to do with the Christian faith in which he
was raised, and it doesn't have to do with the Islamic
faith to which he converted; both great religions. It has
to do with his love for life, his faith in the human spirit,
and his belief in the equality of all people. I see Ali as a
human being whose sense of purpose in life is to help
others. He must lay awake at night, wondering what he
can do to help people, because wherever people are in
need, his priorities are there. He sees children who are
right next to him, but children who are starving in Africa
and threatened by bombing in Iraq are also within the
scope of his imagination. He wants to help everyone,
and he travels at great personal burden and financial
expense to be wherever he's needed. And I say, God
bless him. He makes an enormous difference.

- - - - - - - - - -

RAMSEY CLARK

In this business, we tend to be cynical. Boxing has that effect on people. But when I'm sitting with Mike Katz, Wally Matthews, Larry Merchant, whoever — it can be the most skeptical, cynical guys in boxing — whenever the conversation turns to Ali, it's like a bunch of nuns talking about the Pope.

LOU DIBELLA

ABOVE: *In 1988, Ali was reunited with George Foreman, Joe Frazier, Ken Norton, and Larry Holmes.*
FACING PAGE: *On March 7, 1987, Ali watched Mike Tyson dispose of James "Bonecrusher" Smith in a heavyweight championship unification bout.*

Tyson, as great as he may reign, will never be anywhere near the icon Ali is. There's no comparison. The only thing you cannot give or take away is star quality. One has great physical attributes. The other has star quality. If Ali had to fight in an empty arena, he would have gone on to another profession. Ali was a performer. Ali was a show. Tyson fights because he's a fighter. He has to fight. If Tyson wasn't fighting in the ring, he'd be fighting someplace else. He'd fight you in the parking lot. Whereas, I don't think Ali was ever in a street fight in his life.

SYLVESTER STALLONE

Mike Tyson punches like he's going to crush his opponent's face and cave in his opponent's ribs. But Tyson at his best wouldn't have caught up to the young Ali. And as far as Ali after the exile is concerned — George Foreman punched just as hard as Tyson. And Ali took everything Foreman threw at him, threw back, and knocked George out.

FERDIE PACHECO

When Ali lost, the world mourned. When Mike Tyson lost, outside Don King, nobody shed a tear.

MIKE KATZ

I was the coordinator of Nelson Mandela's trip through the United States in 1990, and I was extraordinarily moved by the sustained love and joy that greeted him from one end of the country to the other. But after a while, it began to wear him down. Every bigshot politician and celebrity wanted a piece of him. They were all grabbing and grasping; and Mandela went through it with incredible grace, but I will tell you, he was unimpressed by the behavior of many of the politicians and so-called superstars that he came in contact with. Then we got to Los Angeles, which is star-studded to begin with, and they turned out every star you can imagine. Mandela was more than tired by then; he was exhausted. We were walking together at yet another fundraising event. Mandela was leaning on me. And all of a sudden, I saw his face light up as I'd never seen it light up before. He looked past me, with a radiant smile. I felt his entire body straighten up and come to life, and almost reverentially he whispered, "Champ." And, of course, walking toward us was Muhammad Ali.

ROGER WILKINS

ABOVE: *With Nelson Mandela in 1990.*
FACING PAGE. TOP: *At the White House with Bill Clinton in February 1996.* BOTTOM: *With Fidel Castro in 1996 after bringing medical supplies to Cuba.*

Muhammad Ali taught us all that, whatever color you are, whatever religion you are, you can be proud of who you are.

- - - - - - - - - - -

BILL CLINTON

I got a plan. Someday I'm gonna hitchhike from New York to California with no money, no clothes except

what I'm wearing, nothing. Then I'm going from California over to Asia, and from Asia to Europe and Africa

and South America. I'm going all around the world with just my face to see how people greet me and take

care of me. I could go just about any place in the world, knock on any door, and people would know me

" I GOT A PLAN "

and let me in. I might even march on foot through Egypt, Israel, Lebanon, all them countries, and tell people

to stop fighting and agree on a peace that's fair to everyone. Some people say that might be dangerous,

but you gotta take risks. Columbus discovered America by sailing around the world when people thought

he'd fall off. We got men on the moon by risking their lives. And then, when my trip is done, I'm going back

around the world the other way. And I'll buy food and clothes for everyone I met before.

MUHAMMAD ALI

FACING PAGE: *"The Greatest" by The Greatest Wall. Ali in China in 1992.*

Ain't life amazing. Twenty-five years ago, they wouldn't let me fight to earn a living. And now they're paying me $100,000 to go to the movies.

— — — — — — — — — —

Muhammad Ali
(REFLECTING ON A $100,000 FEE HE RECEIVED FOR ATTENDING TWO PROMOTIONAL SCREENINGS OF A MADE-FOR-TELEVISION DOCUMENTARY)

Ali did things that nobody did before in life. Never did them after, neither.

— — — — — — — — — —

Earnie Shavers

Everyone has a right to their own opinion.

— — — — — — — — — —

Muhammad Ali

Left: *Ali, in the driveway of his home in Berrien Springs.*

We all love him.

JIMMY CARTER

There will always be another great fighter. There will always be another great baseball player. But there will never be another

Muhammad Ali.

BRYANT GUMBEL

FACING PAGE AND ABOVE: *At the 1996 Atlanta Olympics, Ali received a gold medal to replace his medal from Rome that was lost decades ago. Moments later, he was surrounded by America's "Dream Team."*

On February 7, 1996, I was in the lobby of the ANA-Westin Hotel in Washington, D.C. with Muhammad Ali, Jim Brown, Ralph Boston, and a handful of others. That night, Home Box Office would present a promotional screening of *The Journey of the African-American Athlete*. In anticipation of the event, ten people had been invited to the White House to meet with President Clinton in the Oval Office. My name was on the list, along with Nancy Bronson, whom I'd been dating for six months. The minibus that would take us to the White House was pulling up to the hotel when Seth Abraham, president of Time Warner Sports, approached me with a look of consternation.

"Didn't anybody tell you?"

"Tell me what?"

"Yesterday, the White House took you and Nancy off the guest list. You've been replaced by Zina Garrison and Calvin Hill."

Seth was apologetic. Nancy was accepting. And Muhammad was . . . well, Muhammad was Muhammad.

"Stay by me. I'll get you into the White House."

"Don't waste your time," Paul Costello, Time Warner's point man in Washington, told us. "No one just walks into the Oval Office. In fact, no one gets past the White House gate without advance security clearance. All that will happen is, you'll have to turn around and take a cab back to the hotel."

Which seemed likely. But Nancy and I had nothing to lose, so we boarded the minibus with the others. When we arrived at the first security checkpoint by a wrought-iron gate outside the White House, a guard asked for an identification card from each of us. Five minutes passed. Several limousines drove by. Then the guard returned.

"There's two people who don't have security clearance. Who are Hauser and Bronson?"

Nancy and I raised our hands.

"Come with me, please."

Nancy and I got off the minibus and followed the guard to the security booth, where I pleaded our cause. "I was told on Monday that we'd been approved by the White House. . . . No one told us our names had been taken off the list. . . ."

The guard was polite but unyielding. "I'm sorry; you can't go any further."

At which point, Muhammad joined us.

The guard repeated what he'd just said. "Mr. Ali, this man and this woman don't have security clearance. I'm sure you understand how these things work. They simply can't go any further."

And Muhammad was understanding — "If they don't go, I ain't going."

Unsure as to what to do next, the guard telephoned the White House. Minutes later, an official-looking man with a mustache strode down to the gate to meet us. "What seems to be the problem?" Obviously, he already knew what the problem was, because before I could answer, we were advised, "Look, this is my event. Your names aren't on the list, and that's the end of it. No one without security clearance is allowed past this gate."

"But these are my friends."

"Mr. Ali, you don't understand."

Nancy got back on the minibus, and Paul Costello came over to monitor the proceedings. There followed an explanation about how Barbra Streisand had recently been invited to the White House. *The* Barbra Streisand, who had helped raise millions of dollars for the Democratic party and was a personal friend of the President and Mrs. Clinton. Yet when Ms. Streisand brought someone with her for her appointment with the President, her friend was turned away at the gate.

And Muhammad was duly impressed.

"Did Barbra Streisand whup Joe Frazier?"

"Mr. Ali — "

"Did Barbra Streisand whup Sonny Liston?"

The Man With The Mustache, who I'm sure is a fine public servant and was just trying to do his job, excused himself and returned moments later. "All right; we've got to get this show on the road, so you two [pointing to Nancy and me] can go as far as the reception area, but that's all."

The minibus proceeded to the West Wing of the White House, where we were ushered into a reception area. There was small talk. Several minutes passed. Then The Man With The Mustache reappeared.

"Those of you with security clearance, come with me into the Roosevelt Room. You two [pointing to Nancy and me], stay here."

The members of the group with security clearance were ushered into the Roosevelt Room, directly across the corridor from the Oval Office. Nancy and I stayed in the reception area, settling on a sofa. Inside the Roosevelt Room, various cabinet members, presidential aides, and White House staffers had gathered for a "photo op" with Muhammad.

Except Muhammad wasn't there. He was with Nancy and me in the reception area beneath a painting of "George Washington Crossing the Delaware."

Which is how Nancy and I got into the Roosevelt Room.

"But I'm telling you now," The Man With The Mustache warned. "You are not going into the Oval Office, and I mean it."

And he did mean it.

When the time came to enter the President's office, The Man With The Mustache approached. "You two [Nancy and me], sit over there [pointing to the far side of the conference table]." He waited until we'd followed his command.

"Now, I'd like the rest of you to line up over here."

At which point, I said to Nancy, "Look; there's no way that both of us will make it into the Oval Office. When the others go in, just walk over to Muhammad and take his arm."

"What about you?"

"I'll stay here."

"That's not fair to you."

"Sure it is. I've been to the White House. I already have a photo of me with the President."

"Not in the Oval Office."

"It doesn't matter. You can go into the office for both of us."

Across the corridor, the door to the Oval Office opened; we saw the President of the United States standing there.

The line started to move forward. Nancy got up from the sofa, walked over to Muhammad, and with considerable trepidation took his arm. . . .

The Man With The Mustache walked over to Nancy, and stood in front of her. "Mr. Ali," he importuned. "The President of the United States is waiting for you." And Muhammad walked forward, alone.

Nancy and I watched from a distance as the President greeted his guests. Then the door to the Oval Office closed, and we were left in the Roosevelt Room.

I was disappointed. I won't tell you I wasn't. For a while, we explored our surroundings, which was kind of fun. If you're ever in the Roosevelt Room, I suggest you look at the gold medallion given to Teddy Roosevelt in 1906 when he won the Nobel Peace Prize. Also, check out the bronze sculpture by Alexander Pope, and the portraits of Teddy, Franklin, and Eleanor Roosevelt.

Nancy did her best to put a good face on things. "Tom, this is really very exciting. We're having a wonderful time in Washington with Muhammad. We're in the White House. We saw the President from a few yards away. Don't feel bad for me."

But I did feel bad, for both of us.

Muhammad and the others stayed in the Oval Office for about ten minutes. Then the door to the President's office opened, and they filed out, moving down an adjacent corridor.

Jim Brown . . . Ralph Boston . . . Calvin Hill . . . Zina Garrison. . . .

All but one.

Finally, Muhammad Ali walked out of the Oval Office — leading the President of the United States by the arm toward the Roosevelt Room.

"These are my friends," Muhammad told him.

Bill Clinton smiled, and beckoned us forward with a wave of his arm toward the Oval Office.

"Come on in."

The minutes that followed will remain forever etched in my mind. The President began by asking Nancy her name. Then he turned to me. We chatted briefly; the President was warm and gracious. Eventually, he even called in a photographer. But what I remember most about that afternoon, and always will, is something I've seen many times; something that has been on display for the entire world for almost four decades — the sweetness, the determination, the power, and the magic of Muhammad Ali.

FIGHT CHRONOLOGY

TB:61 KO:37 WD:19 LD:4 KO by:1

TB: Total Bouts / **KO:** Knock Out / **WD:** Won by Decision / **LD:** Lost by Decision / **KO by:** Knocked Out

October 29, 1960
Tunney Hunsaker
WD 6
Freedom Hall,
Louisville, Kentucky

December 27, 1960
Herb Siler
KO 4
Auditorium,
Miami Beach, Florida

January 17, 1961
Tony Esperti
KO 3
Auditorium,
Miami Beach, Florida

February 7, 1961
Jim Robinson
KO 1
Convention Hall,
Miami Beach, Florida

February 21, 1961
Donnie Fleeman
KO 7
Auditorium,
Miami Beach, Florida

April 19, 1961
Lamar Clark
KO 2
Freedom Hall,
Louisville, Kentucky

June 26, 1961
Duke Sabedong
WD 10
Convention Center,
Las Vegas, Nevada

July 22, 1961
Alonzo Johnson
WD 10
Freedom Hall,
Louisville, Kentucky

October 7, 1961
Alex Miteff
KO 6
Freedom Hall,
Louisville, Kentucky

November 29, 1961
Willi Besmanoff
KO 7
Freedom Hall,
Louisville, Kentucky

February 10, 1962
Sonny Banks
KO 4
Madison Square Garden,
New York City

February 28, 1962
Don Warner
KO 4
Convention Hall,
Miami Beach, Florida

April 23, 1962
George Logan
KO 4
Memorial Sports Arena,
Los Angeles, California

May 19, 1962
Billy Daniels
KO 7
St. Nicholas Arena,
New York City

July 20, 1962
Alejandro Lavorante
KO 5
Memorial Sports Arena,
Los Angeles, California

November 15, 1962
Archie Moore
KO 4
Memorial Sports Arena,
Los Angeles, California

January 24, 1963
Charlie Powell
KO 3
Civic Arena,
Pittsburgh, Pennsylvania

March 13, 1963
Doug Jones
WD 10
Madison Square Garden,
New York City

June 18, 1963
Henry Cooper
KO 5
Wembley Stadium,
London, England

February 25, 1964
Sonny Liston
(won WH title) KO 7
Convention Hall,
Miami Beach, Florida

May 25, 1965
Sonny Liston
(retained WH title) KO 1
St. Dominick's Arena,
Lewiston, Maine

November 22, 1965
Floyd Patterson
(retained WH title) KO 12
Convention Center,
Las Vegas, Nevada

March 29, 1966
George Chuvalo
(retained WH title) WD 15
Maple Leaf Gardens,
Toronto, Canada

May 21, 1966
Henry Cooper
(retained WH title) KO 6
Highbury Stadium,
London, England

August 6, 1966
Brian London
(retained WH title) KO 3
Earls Court Stadium,
London, England

September 10, 1966
Karl Mildenberger
(retained WH title) KO 12
Wald Stadium,
Frankfurt, Germany

November 14, 1966
Cleveland Williams
(retained WH title) KO 3
Astrodome,
Houston, Texas

February 6, 1967
Ernie Terrell
(retained WH title) WD 15
Astrodome,
Houston, Texas

March 22, 1967
Zora Folley
(retained WH title) KO 7
Madison Square Garden,
New York City

April 28, 1967
Suspended for
refusing induction into
United States Army

October 26, 1970
Jerry Quarry
KO 3
Municipal Auditorium,
Atlanta, Georgia

December 7, 1970
Oscar Bonavena
KO 15
Madison Square Garden,
New York City

March 8, 1971
Joe Frazier
(for WH title) LD 15
Madison Square Garden,
New York City

July 26, 1971
Jimmy Ellis
KO 12
Astrodome,
Houston, Texas

November 17, 1971
Buster Mathis
WD 12
Astrodome,
Houston, Texas

December 26, 1971
Jurgen Blin
KO 7
Hallenstadion Arena,
Zurich, Switzerland

April 1, 1972
Mac Foster
WD 15
Martial Arts Hall,
Tokyo, Japan

March 31, 1973
Ken Norton
LD 12
Sports Arena,
San Diego, California

June 30, 1975
Joe Bugner
(retained WH title) WD 15
Merdeka Stadium,
Kuala Lumpur, Malaysia

September 29, 1977
Earnie Shavers
(retained WH title) WD 15
Madison Square Garden,
New York City

May 1, 1972
George Chuvalo
WD 12
Pacific Coliseum,
Vancouver, Canada

September 10, 1973
Ken Norton
WD 12
Forum, Inglewood,
California

October 1, 1975
Joe Frazier
(retained WH title) KO 15
Araheta Coliseum,
Quezon City, Philippines

February 15, 1978
Leon Spinks
(lost WH title) LD 15
Las Vegas Hilton,
Las Vegas, Nevada

June 27, 1972
Jerry Quarry
KO 7
Convention Center,
Las Vegas, Nevada

October 20, 1973
Rudi Lubbers
WD 12
Senyan Stadium,
Djakarta, Indonesia

February 20, 1976
Jean-Pierre Coopman
(retained WH title) KO 5
Clemente Coliseum,
Hato Rey, Puerto Rico

September 15, 1978
Leon Spinks
(regained WH title) WD 15
Superdome,
New Orleans, Louisiana

July 19, 1972
Al "Blue" Lewis
KO 11
Croke Park,
Dublin, Ireland

January 28, 1974
Joe Frazier
WD 12
Madison Square Garden,
New York City

April 30, 1976
Jimmy Young
(retained WH title) WD 15
Capital Center,
Landover, Maryland

June 27, 1979
Announced Retirement

September 20, 1972
Floyd Patterson
KO 8
Madison Square Garden,
New York City

October 30, 1974
George Foreman
(regained WH title) KO 8
20th of May Stadium,
Kinshasa, Zaire

May 24, 1976
Richard Dunn
(retained WH title) KO 5
Olympiahalle,
Munich, Germany

October 2, 1980
Larry Holmes
(for WH title) KO by 11
Caesar's Palace,
Las Vegas, Nevada

November 21, 1972
Bob Foster
KO 8
High Sierra Theatre,
Stateline, Nevada

March 24, 1975
Chuck Wepner
(retained WH title) KO 15
Coliseum,
Cleveland, Ohio

September 28, 1976
Ken Norton
(retained WH title) WD 15
Yankee Stadium,
New York City

December 11, 1981
Trevor Berbick
LD 10
QEII Sports Centre,
Nassau, Bahamas

February 14, 1973
Joe Bugner
WD 12
Convention Center,
Las Vegas, Nevada

May 16, 1975
Ron Lyle
(retained WH title) KO 11
Convention Center,
Las Vegas, Nevada

May 16, 1977
Alfredo Evangelista
(retained WH title) WD 15
Capital Center,
Landover, Maryland

The first time I ever saw Muhammad Ali was when I watched his second fight against Joe Frazier with my father. I was five years old, and the only reason I paid attention was because my father was fascinated by what was going on, and being a kid, I wanted to know what was so fascinating to my father. And watching what Ali did that night, the main thing I picked out was, he was smart enough to keep Frazier on the defensive at all times. Frazier was so worried about what Ali was doing that what Frazier did didn't seem to matter. And that made me want to box. Even though I was only five years old, I saw the whole picture right there in front of me. I knew that what Ali was doing was something I could do, if only I could get someone to teach me how to do it.

- - - - - - - - - -

ROY JONES, JR.
(CONSIDERED BY MANY TO BE ALI'S HEIR AS, POUND FOR POUND, THE WORLD'S GREATEST FIGHTER)

174

Photographic references indicated in bold type.

ACKNOWLEDGMENTS

Created and Produced by Opus Productions Inc.

I would like to thank Howard Bingham for agreeing to participate in this project; without his cooperation, this book would never have been possible. I would also like to thank Tom Hauser for believing in this project enough to spend countless hours researching, writing, editing, and negotiating to make sure every detail down to the last period was perfect. A special thanks to Derik Murray and Marthe Love of Opus Productions for giving me the opportunity to do this book and for working tirelessly in its creation. I would like to thank my children for giving me the opportunity every day for the past twenty-eight years to be a father, and enriching my life more than I can say. I would like to thank my wife Lonnie, who took hold of my hand late in life and has been at my side truly for better and for worse. She too, worked many long hours on this book while keeping the family, office, and our lives running smoothly. Last but not least, I would like to give a big, big, thank you to all the friends and fans I have, and have had in this world. Without you, none of this would have been possible. You have given me the opportunity for a most extraordinary life. You've made my life interesting to live and, through it all, you have always believed in me. For that I will always be grateful.

Muhammad Ali

Opus Productions Inc.

President/Creative Director: **Derik Murray**
Vice President, Production: **David Counsell**
Design Director: **Don Bull**
Visual Coordinator: **Joanne Powers**
Photo Researcher: **Dot McMahon**
Electronic Art: **Joseph Llamzon,**
Guylaine Rondeau

Chief Financial Officer: **Jamie Engen**
General Counsel/Photo Permissions: **Ruth Chang**
Marketing Manager: **David Attard**
Sales Representative: **Chris Richardson**
Office Manager: **Catherine Palmer**

Vice President/Publishing Director: **Marthe Love**
Senior Editor: **Brian Scrivener**
Managing Editor: **Jennifer Love**
Publishing Associate: **Wendy Darling**
Editorial Coordinator: **Michelle Hunter**
Publicity Coordinator: **Gillian Hurtig**
Publishing Assistants: **Iris Ho, Allie Wilmink**

Opus Productions would like to extend a special thank you to Muhammad and Lonnie Ali, Thomas Hauser, and Howard Bingham for their uncompromising dedication and invaluable contribution to this project.

Harper Collins Publishers: **Carole Bidnick, Maura Carey Damacion, Ken Fund, Paul Kelly, Jain Lemos, Terri Leonard, Carole Vandermeyde**

Opus Productions would like to acknowledge the following for their assistance:
Colette Aubin; Damon Bingham; Trevor Doull, Sportsbook Plus; Kim Forburger; Jim Forni, Christy Egan, Bradley Printing; Doug Hagart, Sharp Imaging; Barry Kasoff, General Manager of Takarajimasha, Inc.; John Nicolls

Muhammad Ali and Howard Bingham
Robert Mizono

Photo Credits

Principal Photography by Howard Bingham

Cover: **Gregory Heisler**; Courtesy of **Lonnie Ali**: 2; **Allsport/Michael Cooper**: 5, back cover; **AP/Wide World**: 69; **Archive Photos**: 14, 64–65, 67, 97; **Benjamin, Martin**/Black Star: 161; **Bingham, Howard**: front endsheets, 6, 17, 36, 37, 38, 39, 40, 42 below, 43, 51, 52, 53, 58–59, 61, 68, 70, 72, 73, 74–75, 76, 77, 79, 82, 83, 88, 92, 95, 98, 102 above, 103 below, 104 below left and right, 106–7, 110–11, 112, 113, 115, 120, 121, 122, 125, 126 above and below, 127, 128–29, 130, 131, 132–33, 136, 137, 138 all, 140 above and below, 141, 146 above and below, 149 above and below, 150, 153, 154, 156, 158–59, 160, 162, 163 above and below, 164, 166–67, 168, 169, 171; *The Courier Journal*: 10, 13 above and below, 18, 24 above left and right and below right, 25 above; **Drake, James**/*Life Magazine* © *Time Inc.*: 27, 42 above; **Gomel, Bob**/*Life Magazine* © *Time Inc.*: 44, 57 left; **Hamill, Brian**/Photoreporters, Inc.: 142–43; **Gregory Heisler Photography, Inc.**: 144, 145; **Hoepker, Thomas**/Magnum Photos, Inc. : 50, 54, 55, 66, 78; **Iacono, John**/*Sports Illustrated*: 91; **Kalinsky, George**: 84, 124; **Lyon, Danny**/Magnum Photos, Inc.: 80–81; **Millan, Manny**/*Sports Illustrated*: 134–35; **Peskin, Hy**/*Sports Illustrated*: 26; **Regan, Ken**/Camera 5: 87, 98–99, 114–15, 116, 117, 118, 123; Courtesy of **Ronny Paloger**: 9, 25 below; **Scharfman, Herb**/*Life Magazine* © *Time Inc.*: 49, 62; **Schulke, Flip**/Black Star: 28, 31; © **Schulke, Flip**: 8, 30 left and right, 32–33, 34, 35; **Simon, Peter Angelo**/Soho Imageworks, Inc.: 102 below, 103 above, 104 above left and right, 105, back endsheets; **Triolo, Tony**/*Sports Illustrated*: 46–47, 63, 100; **UPI/Corbis-Bettmann**: 24 below left; **UPI/Bettmann**: 21, 41, 48, 56, 57 right, 60, 108, 109, 139; **Waite, David Lee**/Sportschrome: 23

•

F<small>OLLOWING PAGE</small>: *In 1963, Cassius Clay posed with $1 million to emphasize the riches that he believed his ring skills would bring him.*